As a longtime residen~~t~~ ~~~~ ~~~~ ~~~~ ~~~~ ~~~~ ~~~~ ~~~~ l, and state representativ~~e~~ ~~~~ ~~~~ ~~~~ ~~~~ ~~~~ ~~~~ d about this inspirationa~~l~~, ~~~~ ~~~~ ~~~~ ~~~~ ~~~~ ~~~~ ~~~~ ~~~~ ~~~~ ~~~~ as written a very thought-provoking book that details how a ~~church~~ can move from a declining congregation to one on fire for the Lord. The book is easy to read, easy to understand, and is a blueprint for multicultural spiritual success.

Representative Brooks P. Coleman Jr.,
Georgia State Representative, District 97

Few actually have the courage to lead and develop a strategy for change, to engage what they discover with effective, intentional, evangelistic ministry. A must-read if your church is in an urban setting of density and diversity. From the crucible of leading FBC Duluth to become a multicultural church, Dr. Hearn shares key principles to making the transition that every "tribe, language, and nation" gather to worship together. Dr. Hearn explains that the pastor and church must open their eyes and hearts to the leadership of the Spirit to do ministry *with* the diverse people God has surrounded you with, instead of doing ministry for them. Don't miss that great insight for change!

Stephen P. Davis, vice president,
Convention Relations, North American Mission Board

In *Technicolor*, Pastor Mark Hearn delivers a credible, competent, and compelling work—one of the first to chronicle the healthy and ongoing transition of a formerly homogeneous church to living color. More than mere theory, Mark provides real-time explanation rooted in personal experience and a pastor's heart. Having witnessed the support and excitement of First Baptist Duluth congregants firsthand, I believe pastors everywhere will find it an encouraging and motivating guide for their own journeys to the future.

Mark DeYmaz, pastor, Mosaic Church, Little Rock, Arkansas, president of Mosaix Global Network, author of *Building a Healthy Multi-Ethnic Church* and *re:Mix: Transitioning Your Church to Living Color*

I believe this book will become a blessing to many churches. Dr. Mark Hearn is not just writing on the multicultural ministry; he lives in the multicultural ministry!

Samuel Fang, founder/president/CEO, Mainland China Mission International

Technicolor is a fresh look inside the rising reality of urbanization in America and the world. Dr. Hearn's insight toward reaching the community with the gospel, which is meant for every tongue, hits the mark and resonates within the hearts of leaders who are committed to finish the task. *Technicolor* is not just a "nations are coming to us" type book. It helps us to see the ones that the Lord has placed in our pathway, our daily walk.

Rich Fleming, former urban cluster strategy leader for American Peoples Affinity, International Mission Board, Southern Baptist Convention

The places we call home are changing across our homeland. Our nation is truly a melting pot of cultures from around the world, and now the city of Duluth is the prototype of what the entire nation will look like by 2040. This book shows how the cultural journey of change can be a positive influence within a community.

Nancy Harris, mayor, city of Duluth, Georgia

If you ever wondered what it would be like to ride in a time machine, read *Technicolor*. Pastor Mark Hearn takes us on a trip to see what the future looks like, and it is DIFFERENT from today! Dr. Hearn has done a superb job in leading a traditional suburban Baptist church to see multicultural ministry as an opportunity to turn problems and obstacles into unprecedented growth and Kingdom influence. We thank God for our partnership in building the Korean Theological Institute as just one of their many multicultural ministries.

Chuck Kelley, president,
New Orleans Baptist Theological Seminary

What distinguishes *Technicolor* from other books on multicultural ministry is its behind-the-scenes look at one church's intentional efforts to reach and reflect the diverse community it serves. Moving from a predominantly white congregation to one reflecting people of forty nations and counting, First Baptist Church Duluth is a model other churches can learn from. I personally know of no other pastor that has been more committed to making disciples of all nations than Dr. Mark Hearn.

Will Kratt, lead pastor,
Perimeter Pointe Church, Atlanta, Georgia

The experiences and testimonies in this book are heart-touching. This work will open the eyes of churches to see their communities as God sees them. Pastor Mark's love for people is amazing and is reflected in the FBCD church community. I highly recommend every disciple of Christ should read *Technicolor*.

Daniel Kumar, pastor,
Good News Centre, New Delhi, India

Every pastor and every church that is serious about reaching every culture in their community must read this book! Each chapter is filled with biblical principles and real-life examples to reach every people group. My prayer is that as churches put into practice the examples of this book, that our churches on earth would look more like THE CHURCH in heaven . . . red, yellow, black, and white! They are ALL precious in HIS sight!

Fred Luter, pastor, Franklin Avenue Baptist Church, New Orleans, Louisiana, former president, Southern Baptist Convention

A must-read for every church pastor and church member who wants to know how to embrace the ever-growing multiethnic change in America. My friend Mark Hearn tackles the multiethnic realities in his church. He isn't just writing about this topic; he is living it and leading his church well in adapting and making the move to accept all people.

Maina Mwaura, minister and contributor to *Christianity Today*

When we first met in 2003, multicultural ministry was not even a part of Mark's vocabulary! This book is not only a guide and encouragement to all those facing a diaspora movement across the globe, it is a journey of faith and faithfulness from which we may all learn and grow. May his . . . may THIS tribe increase!

David G. Pope, director of operations, Issachar Initiative

I celebrate Dr. Mark Hearn's journey of understanding, appreciation, and passionate embracing of the Great Commission. His thirst and hunger for the harvest of souls began like a mustard seed; it literally started in his own backyard and grew within his local community and church. This stretched him outside his comfort zone all the way to the utmost corners of the world. I pray that you, too, as you read this book, will move outside your comfort zone and become passionate for His Kingdom.

Cornel Potra, Esquire, Potra Law Firm,
Immigration Specialist

Most church leaders find ways to leave a changing community. I can only imagine Mark Hearn's reaction when he learned the local high school in his community had students speaking fifty-seven different languages! Instead of panicking or moving, Mark and his church embraced the diversity. And the rest of the story is, well . . . amazing. Get ready to get a foretaste of heaven. It's all in there in this incredible book, *Technicolor.*

Thom Rainer, president and CEO,
LifeWay Christian Resources, author of
Who Moved My Pulpit? and *I Am a Church Member*

A compelling read for laity and pastors alike who want to see practical examples of how God can work through the challenges of transitioning a one-hundred-plus-year-old fellowship now located in the midst of a multicultural community from a primarily Anglo membership to one that consciously gives deference to all cultures in the community. A mix of personal stories, examples of principles put into practice along with scriptural grounding for actions. This work is filled with keen observations focused on evangelical ministry.

Leland Strange, president and CEO,
Intelligent Systems Corporation
former chairman of deacons, First Baptist Church Duluth

Mark Hearn has captured both the joys and challenges of being a multicultural congregation. He not only writes from a philosophical point of view, but writes from his own personal journey. This is a must-read if you want to lead your congregation to reflect the cultural makeup of your community.

Hugh Townsend, executive director of missions, Gwinnett Metro Baptist Association

One of our beloved Georgia Baptist pastors with the nations in his heart moves to a location populated by the nations of the world. You will be deeply inspired to see how God has used Dr. Mark Hearn and First Baptist Church Duluth to transition its ministry from an established, monolithic, Southern culture community to a multicultural, multilingual, highly diverse community. I highly recommend this book to all who desire ministry to the nations of the world in their own neighborhood.

J. Robert White, executive director, Georgia Baptist Mission Board

TECHNICOLOR

TECHNI COLOR

INSPIRING YOUR CHURCH
TO EMBRACE

▼

MULTICULTURAL MINISTRY

MARK HEARN

B&H
PUBLISHING GROUP
NASHVILLE, TENNESSEE

978-1-4336-9173-7

Published by B&H Publishing Group
Nashville, Tennessee

Dewey Decimal Classification: 261.8
Subject Heading: ETHNOLOGY—UNITED STATES \ ETHNIC
RELATIONS \ CHURCH AND SOCIAL PROBLEMS

1 2 3 4 5 6 7 • 21 20 19 18 17

Dedicated to my partner and advisor in ministry . . .
my precious wife, Glenda.

And to the wonderful congregation of First Baptist
Church Duluth who have traveled this journey alongside us.

Contents

Section Two: The Biblical Practices
of Multicultural Ministry

Foreword

A s I write this, the world is preparing for yet another summer
Olympic games. It's a big event in our home. It's not just that
we love to watch the competition and root for the athletes—
although we enjoy that as well—it's that when we watch the
Olympics together, we celebrate more of the victories than most
families. You see, three of our six kids are from outside of the
United States. Any time athletes from the U.S., China, Ethiopia,
or the Philippines take the field, we're cheering them on. It's
always a lot of fun.

In this way, our family is much like the growing number of
neighborhoods in North America. Think about this. We've heard
for years about the increasing diversity of the United States. By
the year 2050, we've been told more than half of our nation's
population will be from minority ethnic groups. In other words,
the United States will be majority-minority. Politicians have told
us this. Journalists have reported about its ramifications. Pastors
have preached about its impact on the church's mission.

It's easy to miss something very important about this ethnic
transformation: *our kids are already there.* In 2015, the U.S. Census
Bureau reported that 50.4 percent of the 19.9 million children
under the age of five are minorities.[1] The world our kids inhabit
today is a precursor to the nation's even more diverse future. In

fact, in our most populous places, we're already there too. Of the twenty-five most populous counties in the United States, nineteen of them have a majority of non-white people.

The enclaves of our communities built around a single culture in our nation are quickly disappearing. In years past, you and your church may have lived in one. Most likely, you no longer do.

North America is changing. Just a generation or two ago, your church could reach its community by focusing its energies on a single monolithic culture. Our church members could tell their neighbors about Jesus and invite them to our churches easily because they largely shared a worldview.

Those days are gone—and quickly becoming long gone.

In our efforts to push back lostness throughout North America, Southern Baptists have been active in planting churches among ethnic-minority populations. Most years we plant more non-Anglo churches than Anglo churches. In 2016 52 percent of the churches planted by Southern Baptist churches were ethnic-minority churches.

But simply planting churches can't reach all the different people groups that have come to our communities in recent years. As God brings the nations to our doorsteps, established churches—some that have been in our communities for more than a century—will have to do ministry differently, not only to fulfill our God-given mission, but for simple survival.

First Baptist Church of Duluth, Georgia, is on the leading edge of what God is doing to reach our nation's growing diversity. My friend, Pastor Mark Hearn, will share with you in this book about FBC Duluth's ministry in one of the nation's most diverse communities. It's a great story of God transforming a mostly white church into a congregation that's learning to effectively minister cross-culturally.

Today, diversity isn't limited to a suburb of Atlanta. Diversity touches almost every community in our nation. That includes yours. Pastor Mark's journey began when he discovered the fifty-seven languages served in Duluth's public schools. How many languages does your local school district serve? Do you know?

If we're going to continue to reach our communities with the good news about Jesus, we must open up our churches to reach all the ethnicities in them. It won't be easy. It will mean sacrificing our preferences. It will mean learning to communicate in new ways—maybe even learning new languages!

Since 1845 Southern Baptist churches have sent missionaries to every crevice in North America and every corner of the world. And until Jesus returns, we will continue to do that. But in our moment in history—this moment—God has brought the nations to us. The Church has always been called to be on mission cross-culturally, both at home and abroad. But as people arrive at our doorsteps from all over the world, that calling has become critical.

Your church is called to be on mission. We'll pay a steep price if we forgo it.

My friend Russell Moore recently wrote in the *New York Times*, "A congregation that ignores the global church can deprive itself of revival by overlooking those places where the Spirit is working. The thriving churches of American Christianity are multigenerational, theologically robust, ethnically diverse, and connected to the global church. If Jesus is alive—and I believe that he is—he will keep his promise and build his church. But he never promises to do that solely with white, suburban institutional evangelicalism."[2]

God wants to use your church to reach the nations in your backyard. Take in Pastor Mark's wisdom in this book. Apply it to your ministry. Let's see what God will do through your church's faithfulness.

I can't wait to see it!

Kevin Ezell
President, North American Mission Board

▼ ▼ ▼

Technicolor

The Commencement of Multicultural Ministry

Super Bowl Sunday 2010 was my last day as pastor of the Northside Baptist Church in Indianapolis, Indiana. The church conducted a Super Bowl-themed party as my farewell. Our beloved Colts were playing in the big game that year, but they lost to the New Orleans Saints, compounding the sadness of leaving a precious congregation that I had served for the previous eight years.

Indianapolis is known as the "crossroads of America." More interstate highways intersect in Indy than any other metropolitan city. Northside church had experienced the benefit of being the geographical center of America. We had seen new families come from Maine to Mississippi, California to Florida, and everywhere in between. Because of the eclectic nature of our membership, change was a consistent characteristic in our church.

I lived in a suburban community that had relatively little diversity. More than 90 percent of the population was Anglo. But our church was more progressively diverse than the community. Northside had crossed the racial barrier years before my arrival as pastor. During my tenure, we had four African-American men serve as deacons; one of them served as chairman. The church was also blessed to have among its members a church-planting couple from Bangladesh, as well as a seminary graduate from Venezuela. I had the privilege of baptizing the teenage son and daughter of a refugee family from Iran. These were some of my first tastes of multicultural ministry.

Saying "good-bye" is never easy, but our hearts were turning to our future home and our new field of service in Duluth, Georgia. On a cold wintry day in February, the moving truck was packed and we set our sights southward. The First Baptist Church of Duluth owns a missionary residence for the purpose of housing furloughing international missionaries during their stateside assignments. This lovely home was vacant at the time of our move, so the church permitted us to reside there, allowing us the opportunity to sell our home in Indy and find a house to purchase in the local area.

In the midst of a struggling economy, our house in Indianapolis miraculously sold within a month. My wife, Glenda, and I were now fully devoted to finding the new location we would call "home." I was convinced that the search needed to be within the city limits of Duluth. Eventually, we found that house; you know, the one that you can immediately imagine your family gathering in for holiday traditions. Our belongings were brought out of storage and arrived at our new neighborhood. We quickly began to meet our neighbors. To one side of us was a precious cross-cultural couple—he is from Malaysia and she is from Vietnam.

On the other side was a family from India—specifically Andhra Paadesh, a state I had recently visited. Behind us resided a Korean family, and across the street was a household from Zimbabwe. At the end of our street was an oral surgeon from Puerto Rico. Quickly, I learned that my new neighborhood was a microcosm of my new community.

When I was a child, one of my favorite movies was *The Wizard of Oz*. This timeless classic opens with the cinematic effect of black-and-white photography introducing the main character, Dorothy, from a farming community in rural Kansas. Dorothy and her tiny dog, Toto, are carried away by a twister tornado to an unfamiliar, yet beautiful, distant land. When Dorothy opens the door of the farmhouse following the weathered storm, the movie immediately changes from black and white to *technicolor*. The next line in the dialogue has become a famous quote to emphasize stark change in surroundings. Dorothy lowers to her little dog and says, "Toto, I've a feeling we're not in Kansas anymore!"

My new surroundings gave me a Dorothy experience. I was drinking in the rich hues of color in my new community. But there was nothing in my ministry experience that I could compare with this explosion of diversity. I was quickly falling in love with the beautiful mosaic God was creating in this city, but nothing in my past, educationally or experientially, had prepared me to lead a congregation through the needed change to become relevant in a majority-minority community.

I have been a Southern Baptist pastor for thirty-six years. To prepare for ministry, I attended Carson Newman College, a small Southern Baptist school in East Tennessee, where I majored in biblical studies. Following college, I proceeded to the Southern

Baptist Theological Seminary in Louisville, Kentucky, where I received a master of divinity degree with an emphasis in evangelism. Later in my ministry I would complete a doctor of ministry degree from Luther Rice Seminary in Atlanta, with an emphasis in church growth. I have jokingly said for years that with degrees in biblical studies, evangelism, and church growth, my preparations to deal with real-world problems are very limited! None of my wealth of theological training had prepared me for the situation in which I found myself in Duluth.

The primary storyline of *The Wizard of Oz* is the journey on which Dorothy embarks based upon her new surroundings. She does not know much about what she will face, but she marches forward with a sense of purpose. Likewise, I do not want to mislead readers with any pretentious claims of expertise in the subject of multicultural ministry. What you are reading is not a "how-to" manual on becoming a multicultural ministry. Rather, it is the story of a journey—albeit, a journey not yet completed. This account is not intended for emulation, but for inspiration. This journey needs to be replicated throughout every major metropolitan area across America.

As I began to ascertain God's plan for my church and its impact upon the community, I sought mentors and trailblazers who had preceded me in this process. I discovered the writings of Dr. Mark DeYmaz, pastor of Mosaic Church in Little Rock, Arkansas, and the founder of a network of multicultural churches and ministries named Mosaix. His first two books—*Building a Healthy Multi-Ethnic Church* and *Ethnic Blends* (later renamed *Leading a Healthy Multi-Ethnic Church*)—whetted my appetite to learn from practitioners of multicultural ministry. Eventually,

I would lead our entire staff through a book study of *Leading a Healthy Multi-Ethnic Church*. Since reading his works, Mark has become a personal adviser and dear friend.

Soon afterward I learned of Rodney Woo, a Southern Baptist pastor in suburban Houston, and his book, *The Color of Church*. Woo recounts the story of his seventeen-year pastorate at Wilcrest Baptist Church in Alief, Texas, and their transformation from an all-Anglo congregation to a church representing over forty different nationalities. His work connected with me on multiple levels, as he is a pastor from my denominational heritage and his ministry has involved transitioning a monocultural church to reflect its multicultural community.

The Color of Church was published by B&H Publishing Group—my publisher—in 2009. Since that time, Pastor Woo has relocated to the International Baptist Church in Singapore. Unfortunately, very little has been written on the subject of transitioning an existing ministry to a multicultural model since *The Color of Church*. The topic of multicultural church planting is receiving a great deal of attention today. However, there remains a deficiency of publications detailing the struggles and victories of the transitional church. The lack of resources available to me has heightened my desire to chronicle our journey into multicultural ministry for the benefit of fellow sojourners on this wonderful path.

This book is divided into two sections. The first half explains the biblical principles of multicultural ministry. These foundational truths are firmly rooted in God's Word and provide the impetus for action. I now believe that the multicultural church is not merely the will of God for my church, but the will of God for *every* church! I fully appreciate and understand the need for language churches among first-generation immigrants to America. However, the local school system integrates every language group into a singular learning environment. I believe the Church has an even higher calling than education and a more noble purpose—to unite people across cultural and lingual lines and to exalt the name of Jesus and make Him known in the local community.

The last half of the book shares some biblical practices of a multicultural ministry. Many of the things in these chapters were gleaned from fellow journeymen or learned simply by trial and error. However, some of these victories can only be described as God's provisions. My prayer is that by reading this work you will find the inspiration necessary to embark upon your own journey, willing in dependence upon God's guidance to take the challenge to impact all of your local community, and not just the portion that looks and talks the most like you.

SECTION ONE

The Biblical Principles of Multicultural Ministry

▼ ▼ ▼

CHAPTER ONE

Project 57

The Calling of Multicultural Ministry

Then He told them, "These are My words that I spoke to you while I was still with you—that everything written about Me in the Law of Moses, the Prophets, and the Psalms must be fulfilled." Then He opened their minds to understand the Scriptures. He also said to them, "This is what is written: The Messiah would suffer and rise from the dead the third day, and repentance for forgiveness of sins would be proclaimed in His name to all the nations, beginning at Jerusalem. You are witnesses of these things. And look, I am sending you what My Father promised. As for you, stay in the city until you are empowered from on high." (Luke 24:44–49)

I n the fall of 2011 I devised a plan to communicate a ministry-altering statistic with my church. The statistic centered on the number 57. The number first appeared as an emblem no larger than a postage stamp in the church's bulletin. With each passing week, the emblem grew in size and prominence. By week three, there were posters bearing 57 strategically placed all over the church facilities. Yet still there was no explanation to the mystery number. Eventually people began to ask the meaning of the now-obvious two-digit elephant in the room.

What is the significance of this number? I received a variety of suggestions to the now-infamous number puzzle. Some of them had suggested it may have been my first car. No, my first car was not a '57 Chevy. My first car was a '74 Ford Maverick. "Well, maybe it's his favorite steak sauce," some speculated. Actually, my favorite steak sauce is A.1., so it wasn't that either. "Perhaps it's his next birthday." Wrong again; that would have been 53 at the time. I occasionally refer to my glory days on the gridiron as a high school football player. "Could it possibly be his high school football jersey number?" No, that would have been 51! More studious people had calculated that it was the exact number of days until Christmas. Although technically correct, this was still not the purpose of the mysterious number! However, the suggestion that caused me the greatest consternation was that the number somehow represented the average length of my sermons. I had no rebuttal for this position!

My question to the congregants was, *When did you first notice it?* It had actually been in the bulletin and the prayer guide for over a month. It was as if something had happened in plain view before them with no one having called attention to it. Therefore, no one knew if it had any significance to them personally. Some people were afraid to ask. "Well, maybe I missed that Sunday, so I'll ask some other time." Or maybe it was, "I'm ashamed that I don't know. Surely everybody else knows what this 57 is all about. After all, it's out on the church sign for everyone on the highway to see." I challenged the entire church to come on an assigned Sunday to learn the meaning of the mysterious number in the morning message.

The Sunday morning of the reveal I received a phone call from Sunday school members that had taken a class retreat to the north Georgia Mountains. They did not want to be left out of the excitement, so they begged me for the information that would be forthcoming in the morning worship service. Due to the easy access to information on social media, I feared that one small slip could ruin the climactic discovery for all. Therefore, I informed them that the best I could offer would be an immediate phone call after the service. I knew then that the intrigue had created the necessary excitement for maximum impact from the information.

This number had been resonating in me for about a year. Something had been said in my presence that I had been unable to release. I believed it to be a significant calling placed on me as a spiritual leader in our community. And now, I was about to share the source of this number and its impact upon me with my congregation.

57 Languages

In February, I had attended the 2011 "State of the City" address by our mayor and First Baptist church member, Nancy Harris. I desired to support our local mayor and establish myself as a civic-minded leader in the community. In her speech, Mayor Harris gave a statistic that I could not fathom. In sharing about the diversity of the community in which we live, she stated that there are fifty-seven different languages spoken at Duluth High School. I could not imagine this being possible. I didn't know there were fifty-seven languages in the world, much less spoken in my local high school! I immediately went to the Duluth High School website to fact-check the veracity of this claim and I found the following description of Duluth High School: "Duluth High School offers the greatest cultural diversity in the county."

I had been pondering this information for months and praying, "What does that mean for the mission and ministry of the First Baptist Church of Duluth?" This is what God placed on my heart: *Project 57*, a challenge to take the gospel to every language group in our immediate area. This mammoth call to action initiated everything that follows in this book. That day, a line was drawn in the sand, and a commitment made that we will not rest until we learn how to cross language and cultural barriers to share the life-changing message of Jesus Christ.

During the formation stage of this new vision, I had been asked to participate in a cooperative task force that included leaders from our International Mission Board of the Southern Baptist Convention, the North American Mission Board, the Georgia Baptist Convention, local Baptist associations in the metro Atlanta area, and a few local church pastors. The reason for this gathering was to strategically plan how to reach the urban centers, the cities of America. During this four-day meeting, I came up with some *DUI* facts. I know the first thing you think of when you hear "DUI" is "driving under the influence." However, this acronym stands for: *diversity*, *urbanization*, and *immigration*.

The first of area of importance is *diversity*. The 2010 Census reports that 28 percent of Duluth residents were born outside of the United States. The *Gwinnett Daily Post*, on March 18, 2011, ran a front-page story about the 2010 Census declaring that Gwinnett County (my home county) has the largest concentration of Hispanic residents in the entire state of Georgia, larger than any other county by far. Over one hundred sixty-two thousand Hispanics call Gwinnett County their home. Twenty percent of the entire state Hispanic population is found in my home county. This is a 250-percent increase since the last decade census in the year 2000.

During the turn of the century, Duluth was quickly becoming one of the most diverse places in America. Duluth is now home to the eighth largest concentration of South Asian people in all of Georgia, the fourth largest concentration of Chinese people, the third largest concentration of South Americans, and the largest concentration of Korean people in our state! During the past decade, the world had fallen in love with Duluth. And now I was falling in love with the world in Duluth.

One of the first international members of First Baptist Church, Titi Esho, from Nigeria, sent an encouraging e-mail to me as we embarked upon this new journey:

> Pastor, I'm not surprised people from many countries are flocking to First Baptist Church Duluth, because there's something special and unique about the church. First, there's the presence of God, and where God's presence is, there is love and peace and fulfillment. Second, there is a true acceptance and friendship, and it is very easy for a foreigner to blend. I went to a couple of churches

before I chose First Baptist, and none of them measured up to my expectation. I believe First Baptist Duluth truly preaches the Word of God and they practice what they preach. God is doing a wonderful thing at First Baptist Church of Duluth.

My prayer has been that we will live up to those lofty words. The second DUI point of emphasis is *urbanization*.[3] The Southern Baptist Convention's International Mission Board reports that over half of the world currently lives in cities. People are congregating in the urban centers across our planet. Just fifty years ago, that number was less than a third. By the year 2050, it will be more like two-thirds. There is an urbanization of society taking place like never before in the history of our planet. People are flocking to the urban centers of the world.

Atlanta is the largest city in the southern United States. My city of Duluth is a nearby suburb of Atlanta. In the 1980s, Duluth was a sleepy little bedroom community. Many residents were part of multigenerational families that had made Duluth their home for a long, long time. By the 1990s, Duluth had become the "up and coming" place for palatial homes and upper-class neighborhoods. Professional athletes and business executives moved their families to this new hot spot. With the turn of the century came a new chapter to Duluth. Many credit Atlanta hosting the 1996 Olympic Games as the catalyst for the suburban communities receiving extraordinary international attention. The world literally moved to Duluth en masse!

The "I" of DUI, stands for *immigration*.[4] The United States has always been the great immigration society—the great melting pot. There were 35 million immigrants from 1780 to 1924. These were predominantly Europeans moving to the Americas for religious freedom. Seventy-five percent of the immigrants during that time period were Protestants. There were Methodists, Baptists, Episcopalians, and Lutherans, most of them from Central and Northern Europe.

However, there is a modern immigration that is taking place at a much faster rate. The last immigration swell saw 35 million come over a nearly 250-year time frame. There were 35 million immigrants from 1970 to 2005—a million immigrants a year. The vast majority of them are *not* Protestant. As a matter of fact, they are Muslim, Buddhist, and Hindu. Many of them struggle with the English language. Forty to sixty-five percent of them do not speak English when they arrive.

Because the first port of entry into America for this new wave of immigrants is a major city, our urban centers are becoming filled with rich ethnic blends. I have seen demographic predictions that in the next twenty-five years every major city in America will become at least 60 percent non-Anglo. This means that there will be no ethnic majority in the United States. The statistical term for this status is "majority-minority." This future ethnic reality in American cities is a current reality in my city of Duluth. My city has been majority-minority since the 2010 census, with the Anglo population being about 42 percent and the rest being a genuine mosaic of cultures.

Churches in America are going to become extinct, or at least severely crippled, unless we learn how to minister in a multicultural society. This truth is even more immediate for me and my arena of ministry. My church would soon be totally irrelevant to our community if we chose not to pursue a process of crossing cultural barriers.

Language is an extreme barrier to the gospel in the new immigration phenomenon. Like many churches in our area, we offer English classes during the week. For many people, this is their first exposure to our church. Classes are taught by highly dedicated, extremely compassionate volunteers who see the rich rewards of assisting these new residents in an essential life skill. Recently, we have been convicted that part of being multicultural is also being multilingual. Therefore, we also offer Spanish language classes and Korean language classes. Learning to converse with our neighbors has been a rewarding process.

Does the Word of God give us instruction on how to reach such a multiethnic society? I have found that the secret is found in a small but incredibly important biblical phrase: *all nations*. These two words unlock what God would have us do until He comes.

All Nations

Old and New Testament alike have *all nations* texts. In order to understand what this phrase really means, we need to first understand what it doesn't mean. Let's start all the way back in the Old Testament, in the book of Genesis, chapter 12, and the promise that was made to Abraham:

> The LORD said to Abram: "Go out from your land, your relatives, and your father's house to the land that I will show you. I will make you into a great *nation*. I will bless you, I will make your name great, and you will be a blessing. I will bless those who bless you, I will curse those

who treat you with contempt, and all the *peoples* [nations] on earth will be blessed through you." (Gen. 12:1–3, emphasis mine)

God promised Abraham that He would make of him a great nation. But what did this promise mean? Did God mean that He would give Abraham a geographical territory? Did God intend for Abraham to become a king or a president with diplomatic clout in the global community? When God said that He would bless "all the nations," was He talking about specific governments? What exactly was God referring to? In the book of Galatians, Paul refers back to the Abrahamic promise. Galatians 3:6 says:

Just as Abraham believed God, and it was credited to him for righteousness, so understand that those who have faith are Abraham's sons. Now the Scripture foresaw that God would justify the Gentiles by faith and told the good news ahead of time to Abraham, saying, *All the nations will be blessed through you.* (emphasis mine)

All nations, according to the Abrahamic promise, did not mean national governments. It referred to something different. Obviously, the reference to Abraham's blessing is not a reference to the 195 currently recognized nations of the world. Thus, we have seen what this phrase does *not* mean. But what does it mean?

Perhaps our best clue comes from the Great Commission in Matthew 28:19–20:

"Go therefore and make disciples of *all nations*, baptizing them in the name of the Father and of the Son and of the

Holy Spirit, teaching them to observe everything I have commanded you." (emphasis mine)

The word used in the original language here is the word *ethne*. From it, we derive our English words *ethnic* and *ethnicity*. I believe this gives us a clue into what the Bible means by all nations. The word *nations* refers, not to geopolitical societies, but to ethnicities; *nations* refers to people groups.

People Groups

Scholars now agree that this word is in reference to ethnolinguistic groups. In other words, a nation is a group of individuals who share a common language, a common religion, a common occupation, a common class, or a common caste. The International Mission Board of the Southern Baptist Convention has identified 11,659 people groups—people who share a common language and culture—of which more than half (6,744), are considered "unreached."

An unreached people group is one with less than 2 percent of its population identified as believers in the Lord Jesus Christ. More than half of the world's people groups are unreached. Among unreached people groups, more than half of them (3,789) are "unengaged" unreached people groups. This means they do not have a Christian witness or missionary assigned to take the gospel to them. In total, then, more than one-fourth of all the people groups on this planet do not know the gospel and have never heard it in their own language.

All nations refers to all of the people groups of the planet. To put this on the bottom shelf for us Southerners, it simply means, "all y'all." God is incredibly inclusive. He says, "All y'all are invited." Have you ever invited someone to your home and said, "All y'all come"? *All nations* is "all y'all"!

The Magnitude of All Nations

Many believers will claim they know the gospel is for all people, but do we act as if God wants to reach all of the people groups on this planet? I once heard a missionary friend exclaim, "Why should anyone hear the gospel twice until everyone has heard it once?"

That has not always been a popular concept, even going all the way back to the Old Testament. Do you remember the story of Jonah? Jonah tried to escape this principle. Jonah was told to go and preach to Nineveh. Remember the response of the prophet? "He got up and fled to Tarshish from the LORD's presence" (Jonah 1:3). He tried to run away from God! How's *that* working for you, Jonah?

I observe people all the time who are trying to run away from God's plan, God's purpose, and God's work in their lives, saying, "It's too hard" or "It's too complicated" or "I don't understand it." Jonah tried to escape God's heart for all nations.

Peter tried to debate this concept. In Acts 10–11, Peter was on a rooftop, praying at noon, like he did every day. He saw heaven open up, and a sheet came down with animals that were unlawful for him to eat by Jewish law. A voice from heaven said, "Eat!" I imagine Peter began to stutter: "But, but, but . . ." God repeated this vision three times. God was revealing to Peter that his narrow view of acceptance was completely wrong. Peter learned the lesson. In Acts 10:34, the Bible says, "Then Peter began to speak: 'In truth, I understand that God doesn't show favoritism, but in *every nation* the person who fears Him and does righteousness is acceptable to Him'" (emphasis mine).

Peter, by God's grace, got it! Later in Acts 11, there was a great debate going on as to whether the gospel was only for the Jewish people or for all people. Peter became the great debater and testified, "God showed me." For some people today, it will take a vision from heaven for them to realize the gospel is indeed for every people group.

Jonah tried to escape this principle. Peter tried to debate this principle. Paul, who called himself an "apostle to the Gentiles" (nations) in Galatians 2:8, just tried to explain it. The clearest explanation of the gospel in the entire Word of God is found in the book of Romans. Many people use these passages to share the gospel. It is commonly referred to as the "Romans Road" of salvation. Romans 3:23: "All have sinned and fall short of the glory of God"; Romans 6:23: "The wages of sin is death, but the gift of God is eternal life through Jesus Christ our Lord"; Romans 5:8–9: "God demonstrated his love toward us in that while we were yet sinners Christ died for us"; Romans 10:9–10: "If you confess with your mouth the Lord Jesus and believe in your heart that God has raised him from the dead you will be saved."

The book of Romans is indeed the doctrinal treatise of the author of the majority of the New Testament. The apostle Paul begins and ends this book by pointing out the inclusiveness of the gospel. The prologue, in Romans 1:5, says, "We have received grace and apostleship through Him to bring about the obedience of faith among *all the nations*, on behalf of His name . . ." (emphasis mine). The last chapter reasserts this sentiment; Romans 16:26 says the mystery of God is "now revealed and made known through the prophetic Scriptures, according to the command of the eternal God, to advance the obedience of faith among *all nations*" (emphasis mine). The "Romans Road" begins with the nations and ends with the nations. Clearly the apostle Paul wanted the church to know that the gospel is intended for every people group.

The Manifestation of All Nations

What happens when the gospel truly goes out to all people groups? The first result is that the nations will *look*. Luke 12:30–31 reads, "For the Gentile world eagerly seeks all these things, and your Father knows that you need them. But seek His kingdom, and these things will be provided for you." This is a reference to a worldwide search for truth. Today there is a hunger for truth like possibly never before in the history of humanity. People are searching for something real. People are desperately searching for truth. The Bible claims that when the nations, those who have never heard the truth, hear truth, they will look into it. Truth, by its very nature, is attractive!

The second result is that they will *listen*. Some fear that people will not listen to them. There is a story of a concert violinist whose playing had a hypnotic effect on all who heard. Patrons would sit through entire concerts expressionless, as in a trance. The virtuoso found that his playing had similar effects on animals. Every time he played, his dog and his cat were spellbound. The violinist wondered if his powers would transcend to wild beasts in their natural habitat. With some degree of confidence, he planned a trip to the jungles of Africa and took his trusted violin. Upon arrival, he immediately planned a trip to a jungle clearing and set up for an impromptu concert. Within moments of his first melodic notes, wild animals began to gather in docile submission; a lion, a gorilla, and an elephant were among the initial attendees. Before long, the clearing was filled with a variety of dangerous animals, all listening to the violinist. Suddenly, a second lion appeared and announced his presence with a great roar and proceeded to maul and eat the gifted musician. The original lion asked his fellow lion, "Why did you do that?" The second lion cupped his hand over his ear and responded loudly, "Huh?"

Many fear that they will be publicly mauled and possibly devoured if they boldly proclaim Christ to people of another ethnicity. The Bible says that if we will share the gospel with all the nations, they will listen! Second Timothy 4:17 says, "But the Lord stood with me and strengthened me, so that the proclamation might be fully made through me, and all the Gentiles might hear." When you tell them, they will listen!

Finally, when we bring the gospel to the nations, they will *live*. In the book of Revelation, we have a beautiful picture of a heavenly worship service. Imagine all the people of God—from all the peoples of the world—gathered around the throne.

> When He took the scroll, the four living creatures and the 24 elders fell down before the Lamb. Each one had a harp and gold bowls filled with incense, which are the prayers of the saints. And they sang a new song: You are worthy to take the scroll and to open its seals; because You were slaughtered, and You redeemed people for God by Your blood *from every tribe and language and people and nation.* (Rev. 5:8–9, emphasis mine)

Lord, who will not fear and glorify Your name? Because You alone are holy, for *all the nations* will come and worship before You because Your righteous acts have been revealed. (Rev. 15:4, emphasis mine)

Then I saw a new heaven and a new earth, for the first heaven and the first earth had passed away, and the sea no longer existed. I also saw the Holy City, new Jerusalem, coming down out of heaven from God, prepared like a bride adorned for her husband. Then I heard a loud voice from the throne: Look! God's dwelling is with humanity, and He will live with them. They will be His people, and God Himself will be with them and be their God. (Rev. 21:1–3)

Heaven is filled with people from every nation. When the gospel was presented to them they were willing to look into it, they listened intensely, they received Christ, and they will experience everlasting life!

The Motivation of All Nations

Every church I have ever been affiliated with claims to be a loving church. I have never known of a church of any size, denomination, or demographic that has not thought of themselves as loving. I am not labeling the modern church as loveless, but perhaps our modern notion of love is not enough to accomplish this task!

I read a very awkward illustration of this truth. Imagine that two ocean liners collided in the midst of the sea and began to sink with thousands of non-swimmers on board. You and a team began rescue operations. You were saving as many as you could, and then you began to hear the cries from the other ocean liner. "Come over here and help us." If you continued to work as diligently as possible at your current location without heeding the distant cries, would that have been due to a lack of love? The answer is obviously "NO." It is because you are busy doing something good. You are doing something effective. You might sense God in what you are currently doing. Love is needed to initiate work. However, love is not adequate to move to a new field of influence. Many times, the enormity of the task colors decision-making.[5]

Love is insufficient because the only real incentive has to be from the Lord. International Mission Board President David Platt, in his book entitled *Radical Together,* devotes an entire chapter to the concept that believers are living and longing for the end of the world. Dr. Platt shares from Mark 13:10 and Matthew 24:14: "This good news of the kingdom will be proclaimed in all the world as a testimony to all nations. And then the end will come." The Bible claims that when we take the gospel to all the people, the end will come. Jesus won't return until all nations have had a chance to hear the good news. Platt states, "Satan must have this verse plastered all over the walls of hell as a warning!"[6] When all the people groups have heard about God's grace, then Jesus is going to return!

The Method of All Nations

For some of you, reading this is like putting together a Rubik's Cube. You understand *all nations* in principle, but have no idea what it would look like in practice. The first key to understanding methodology is a realization of *the importance of heart language.* I have been recently taught that by the age of four to six years, children have developed a value system. This value system is stored in a part of the brain that is triggered by the language spoken to them as a young child. Have you ever heard someone's native language referred to as his "mother tongue"? This is the language that one has heard since infancy. Therefore, it is very difficult—though not totally impossible—to make a value-based decision, such as accepting the gospel, if not presented in one's native language.

Many American churches are doing an outstanding job of embracing immigrants and giving them key life-skill training, including teaching them English. This is an essential asset to living in the United States. However, to care for these people groups on a deeper spiritual plane will require taking the message of Jesus Christ to them in a way that they can make a decision that is beyond the cognitive level of merely understanding the message, moving to a more evaluative, heartfelt judgment.

An example of this principle is found in the book of Acts, on the day of Pentecost. The miracle that took place at Pentecost was when the apostles began to speak in languages they didn't know. "How is it that we hear, each of us, in our own native language?" (Acts 2:8). It was when they heard the gospel in their mother tongue that they began to respond en masse.

The second key to implementing methodology is *understanding the importance of Christ's life.* The one common thread that draws us together is not culture, but Christ. Early in my ministry at First Baptist Church, we went through a rebranding process that included developing a new logo that would reflect our mission and ministry. The logo chosen by our church staff was a modern design with multicolored shapes converging to form a cross. The multiple shapes represent different age groups and generations. The multiple colors represent different ethnicities and people groups. The unifying factor that brings together multiple generations and multiple ethnicities is the cross of Jesus. "There is salvation in no one else, for there is no other name under heaven given to people, and we must be saved by it" (Acts 4:12). The reason we gather every Sunday morning is the commonality of our faith. Jesus is the ultimate unifier!

This methodology also emphasizes the *importance of home location.* "You will be My witnesses in Jerusalem, in all Judea and Samaria, and to the ends of the earth" (Acts 1:8). Jerusalem is our home missions or local mission field, Judea is our regional mission field, Samaria is our national mission field, and then the ends of the earth are our international mission fields.

Luke the physician wrote both Acts 1:8 and Luke 24:47: ". . . and repentance for forgiveness of sins would be proclaimed in His name to all the nations, beginning at Jerusalem." God will touch all of the nations, beginning with the nations in our local region—Jerusalem. Then God will touch the nations in our Judea, our Samaria, and ultimately, to the ends of the earth. It all begins with reaching the people groups whom God has placed immediately around us. We have such a richness of people groups in the Duluth area. Therefore, Project 57 is a battle cry! Simply stated, Project 57 is:

> We will find a way to communicate the gospel to every people group within reach of First Baptist Church Duluth.[7]

Critics have deemed this goal unachievable and some have scoffed at the attempt. But I believe that it is the biblical call of God, not only for my church, but for every church!

Obedient to God's Will

The following chapters are the story of one church's pursuit of this calling. It is the account of a monocultural congregation's metamorphosis into a multicultural ministry. This must all begin with a clear understanding that this journey is the will of God! The intent is not to have anyone validate our path or even to emulate our path. However, I offer this rendering of the journey to educate future travelers, to help them learn from our mistakes, and to call them to follow the leadership of God's Spirit in reaching all the nations.

▼ ▼ ▼

CHAPTER TWO

More than Purple Bags

The Community of Multicultural Ministry

> *Therefore, brothers, since we have boldness to enter the*
> *sanctuary through the blood of Jesus, by a new and liv-*
> *ing way He has opened for us through the curtain (that is,*
> *His flesh), and since we have a great high priest over the*
> *house of God, let us draw near with a true heart in full*
> *assurance of faith, our hearts sprinkled clean from an evil*
> *conscience and our bodies washed in pure water. Let us*
> *hold on to the confession of our hope without wavering,*
> *for He who promised is faithful. And let us be concerned*
> *about one another in order to promote love and good*
> *works, not staying away from our worship meetings, as*
> *some habitually do, but encouraging each other, and all the*
> *more as you see the day drawing near. (Hebrews 10:19–25)*

L ess than a month from the time that my wife and I relocated to Duluth, our home in Indianapolis was sold. And so the search began for a new residence in our new hometown. The First Baptist Church owns a missionary house that until that time had been primarily used by furloughing missionary families as they took respite during stateside assignments. We were grateful that the missionary house was vacant at the time of our move and provided Glenda and me a place to stay while we searched for our new home.

The suburbs of Atlanta are growing exponentially. But I thought that if I was to be effective as the pastor of First Baptist Church Duluth, I needed to make my home in the city limits of Duluth. During a multicultural church conference I had attended in California, I heard Dr. Wayne Schmidt, general superintendent of the Wesleyan Church, make this statement: "Pray to be called to a community to spend a lifetime, not just called to a church to spend your efforts."[8] This statement resonated within me, and I began to pray that God would allow us to live in the city of Duluth.

I realized that I am serving church members who lived in neighboring communities of Lawrenceville, Suwanee, Buford, Sugar Hill, and Norcross, but there was just something about being the pastor of First Baptist Church in Duluth that gave me a desire to live inside the city of Duluth. Little did I know the difficulty this search would generate. It was nearly impossible to find a home within our price range that was not a "fixer-upper." Tools and my hands do not fit well together. We were trying to find *the* home we could purchase, and it was a long, six-month process. Finally, someone informed us about a subdivision called the "Highlands at Duluth." There were eleven new homes that were for sale. On a Saturday, Glenda and I went there, and we toured all eleven homes. The following Monday, we made the first offer for any home in the subdivision. It was on the first home we had viewed.

A sign outside the neighborhood entrance reads, "Welcome to the city of Duluth." Alas, we own a home and are going to live inside the city limits of Duluth! At the loan closing, Glenda and I received the keys to our new purchase and were informed of our new address. We were the proud owners of the home at 1741 Hickory Path Way . . . Suwanee! What?! I cried out, "Lord, that's just not fair!"

I began lamenting this disturbing news with my friend, Duluth Mayor Nancy Harris. I told Mayor Nancy, "It's just not right. I live inside the city limits of Duluth. I pay Duluth taxes. Yet I have this Suwanee address." She shared with me that different entities draw their boundaries in different ways. The postal service draws it one way. The school system draws it another. The city government draws it yet another way. "Rest assured," she encouraged, "you live inside the city limits of Duluth!"

I asked the mayor, "How will anyone know that I live in Duluth? Our children are grown, so we're not affiliated with any school system. Help me find a way that identifies me beyond any shadow of a doubt as Duluthian!" She calmly asked, "What day is the trash taken out in your neighborhood?" I said, "It's taken out on Wednesdays." In the city of Duluth, the trash is collected on Wednesdays. Rather than pay a city tax for this service, the local government sells hideous-looking purple garbage bags at the local grocers. These bags bear the city seal and anything placed in any other receptacle is not to be retrieved on trash day. Mayor Harris said, "Every time you put those ugly, purple garbage bags in front of your house, you are indicating to the community, 'I am a Duluthian.'"

More than Purple Bags

I thought to myself, *There has to be something more to being a part of this community than just purple garbage bags.* Bill Willits, the small group pastor at North Point Community Church, is a self-proclaimed Starbucks addict. One day on a typical Starbucks stop, Willits saw a sign that read, "Create community. Make a difference in someone's day."

He reasoned, "What could Starbucks be doing to create community and make a difference in someone's day?" An inviting brochure was in easy view at the cash register next to the outlandish claim. Willets picked up the brochure, and began to read: "When you work at Starbucks, you can make a difference in someone's day by creating an environment where neighbors and friends can get together and recount while enjoying a great cup of coffee."[9]

Creating Community

How does one create community? Starbucks is trying to create community around a cup of coffee. Some people say you can create community by competition. After all, in Georgia, we have the Bulldog nation (followers of the University of Georgia athletics programs), and we have the Yellow Jacket nation (followers of Georgia Tech athletics programs). Our congregation is strongly represented by both groups. As a matter of fact, there are congregants who are of the Crimson Tide variety (University of Alabama fans). There are Tigers of all types—from Alabama (Auburn

University fans), from Louisiana (Louisiana State University fans), and from South Carolina (Clemson University fans).

As a matter of fact, when our church gathers on Sunday morning, there are Bulldogs, Yellow Jackets, Crimson Tide, and Tigers of all varieties all under the same roof. Moreover, they're being led by a Hokie preacher (fan of Virginia Tech)! Competition does not typically unite; it tends to divide.

Others attempt to create community around causes. But who gets to determine which causes are worthy of our attention and how are we to strategically address them? That is why we have political parties: a Republican Party, a Democratic Party, a Libertarian Party, etc. Lengthy debates are held to showcase how little we agree upon and how there is no unanimity as to how we address life's most difficult causes. As is the case with competition, causes do not necessarily unite us; they tend to divide us.

What about being united in our community, around our shared culture? If we have the same language, and we have the same background, and the same heritage, perhaps this will provide the impetus to unite us. However, one can drive down Highway 120 where our church is located and find Korean churches, Hispanic churches, and Anglo churches. Culture has not united the church in America; it has divided the church in America!

Everyone approaches cultural diversity from a Genesis 11 mind-set or a Micah 4 mind-set.

> At one time the whole earth had the same language and vocabulary. As people migrated from the east, they found a valley in the land of Shinar and settled there. (Gen. 11:1–2)

Isn't that interesting? Everybody spoke the same language. They had a commonality of heritage. They all came from the same place. Yet, they decided they were going to build their own way to God. How did that work out for them? God scattered humanity, confused their languages, and rejected their idolatrous path to Him.

In Micah 4, we see a totally different approach.

In the last days the mountain of the LORD's house will be established at the top of the mountains and will be raised above the hills. Peoples will stream to it, and many nations will come and say, "Come, let us go up to the mountain of the LORD, to the house of the God of Jacob. He will teach us about His ways so we may walk in His paths." For instruction will go out of Zion and the word of the LORD from Jerusalem. (Micah 4:1–2)

What Holds Us Together?

These are two completely different approaches. One promotes a commonality of culture that brings people together claiming, "We can achieve God." The other promotes a diversity of culture that comes together for the sole purpose of proclaiming, "We will worship God."

A group of church leaders in our congregation were tasked with studying how we can create genuine community at First Baptist Church of Duluth. This was not accomplished in a weekend retreat setting; the eight-person team met weekly for five months wrestling with the assignment. The team represented the deacons (including the past three chairmen), members of the stewardship and personnel committees, and select Sunday school teachers. This group was a genuine cross section of the church.

This eclectic team's first proposal was a fresh mission statement for our church. They desired to write something simple enough that a fourth grader could comprehend it, short enough that anyone could memorize it, and stimulating enough that the congregation could rally behind it. The consensus of their work produced the following: "To be a united community of faith that loves, reaches, and disciples all people for Jesus Christ."

How does one produce a united community of faith? You cannot produce a united community with a cup of coffee. You cannot produce a united community around competition. You cannot have a united community around a cause, or based upon a culture. The only way to unite as a community of faith is around Jesus Christ. He is the reason we gather! The commonness of our faith is what allows us to be a united community. Diversity remains in competition, causes, and cultures; unity is found in the gospel of Jesus Christ.

Our church needed this rallying statement. And our *community* needed to see it put to practice. This statement provided something to buy into. Many responded immediately with desires to be a part of the movement. The question with any mission statement is: How do you go about accomplishing the task? Hebrews 10 instructs the church on how to become a united community of faith. There are three principles in this passage that all begin with the phrase *let us*.

Held Together by Faith

What draws us together is not fun, football, food, or fellowship; it is faith. Verses 19–21 tell us the *subject* of our faith. Our faith is based upon a "new sacrifice." The word *new* is a unique word in the New Testament. This is the only time it appears in the entire Word of God. It is a word that was used in relation to the sacrificial system of worship in that day.

If one literally translated the word, it would mean "freshly slaughtered." When a sacrifice was new, it had been freshly slaughtered. The Bible declares there has been a new sacrifice. This new sacrifice has been made on our behalf. At Jesus' death, the temple curtain—the veil between the Holy Place and the Holy of Holies—was torn from top to bottom.

This veil was comprised of three colors: blue, scarlet, and purple. Blue represents heaven and all that is God. Scarlet represents humanity. The name of the first man God created, *Adam*, is the Hebrew word for humanity, and is very similar to the word for red or ruddy. Purple is the perfect combination of blue and red. Jesus is God and became man, the perfect combination of blue and red! The entrance to the very presence of God passes through the purple path of Jesus Christ. He is not the best way to God—He is the only way to God!

On the day of Jesus' death, the earth quaked and this curtain was torn. It was ripped in two, not opened but torn, because God had made this provision. He had made a perfect passageway by which imperfect man could approach a holy God, and this way is through His Son. Jesus said, "I am the way, the truth, and the life. No man comes to the Father except through Me" (John 14:6). Jesus is the subject of our faith!

We also see the *sincerity* of our faith in this passage. We are commanded to draw near to Christ with a true heart. The word *true* is a word that means sincere, or more literally, genuine. This implies that there are people who will attempt to draw near to Him with an *insincere* heart.

Romans 10:9 states, "If you confess with your mouth 'Jesus is Lord,' and believe in your heart that God has raised Him from the dead, you will be saved." I believe there are many people who have done one and not both of these requirements for salvation. There are people who have said it and never believed it, and there are people who believed it and never said it. The requirement is a sincere heart that not only says, "Jesus is the Lord of my life," but truly and genuinely knows that Jesus is the one and only way to live in the presence of God. What draws us together is our faith!

This is how people from forty different nations and at least fifteen different language groups gather on Sunday mornings at First Baptist Church. We have one thing in common: our faith. In the midst of our diversity, we gather to experience the presence of the Creator of the universe and hear how He desires to impact each of us personally!

Held Together by Hope

I heard a story about a hefty lady who had a fall at the church. No one ever wants to see someone fall. However, this large lady had a husband who was about a fourth of her size. She became somewhat upset that he was not coming immediately to her rescue and said, "Aren't you going to help me up?" He responded and said, "I am, just as soon as I find out where to take hold of."

There are a lot of people at church trying to figure out "where to take hold of." Pundits talk about holding on to our heroes or holding on to our good habits or holding on to our past or holding on to the way things used to be or the way in which we dreamed they once were; the Bible, on the other hand, says to hold on to your hope!

First Peter 3:15 says, "Be ready to give a defense to everyone who asks you a reason for the hope that is in you" (NKJV). Be ready to defend your hope in a world that doesn't understand hope. A familiar hymn sung in church reminds us, "My hope is built on nothing less than Jesus' blood and righteousness." Faith may get us to the church, but hope is what keeps us there. Hope is what keeps us strong in our faith.

As long as one holds to hope, they have security. "They went out from us, but they did not belong to us; for if they had belonged to us, they would have remained with us. However, they went out so that it might be made clear that none of them belongs to us" (1 John 2:19). I believe John learned this principle by watching the ministry of Jesus. Near the end of Jesus' ministry, He observed those who had lost hold of their hope.

"But there are some among you who don't believe." (For Jesus knew from the beginning those who would not believe and the one who would betray Him.) He said, "This is why I told you that no one can come to Me unless it is granted to him by the Father." From that moment many of His disciples turned back and no longer accompanied Him. Therefore Jesus said to the Twelve, "You don't want to go away too, do you?" (John 6:64–67)

People let go in life because they have lost hope! The world is asking with Job, "Where then is my hope? Who can see any hope for me?" (Job 17:15). People are searching for the kind of hope they can hold on to!

I recall as a young boy an occasion when my dad dropped me off at a sporting goods store to do some shopping. This was a great place for me to spend some time while Dad had errands to do. While performing these errands, Dad's car broke down. This was before the days of cell phones, which meant there was no way of contacting me. I remained perfectly content, roaming through the sporting goods store having a great time. When Dad finally arrived, hours later, I came skipping out of the store and bounced my way into the car. Thinking that he needed to explain his extremely tardy arrival, Dad asked, "Weren't you worried?" I said, "Why would I be worried? You said you'd come for me!"

I trusted my father! Even though I didn't know the reason for the delay, I was still holding on to hope. As believers in Jesus we should be able to live life with confidence because of the hope that is in us. There have been many times in my spiritual walk when I did not understand the reasons or the ramifications of what I was going through. However, I fully trusted my Father in heaven, and my hope was securely placed upon Him!

Held Together by Love

In Hebrews 10:24 we are introduced to a special kind of love. The English word "love" is the translation for a variety of words in the Greek language. There is the Greek word *eros*, from which we get the word *erotic*, which means a sensual kind of love. There is the Greek word *philia*, the root of the word "Philadelphia" (the city of brotherly love), which means a sibling kind of love. The word used here in Hebrews is *agape*, a word that means a God-type of love, the Savior's love.

Agape means doing what is best for others without any regard for self. When Jesus died on the cross, He did so out of His great love for us. He did what was best for the world without any regard for Himself. The Bible instructs us as believers to emulate this type of love for the world.

I remember a radio advertisement several years ago that said, "When you believe in people, word gets around." I think that would be a great slogan for a church. When the community observes the church and concludes, "They don't care about themselves as much as they care about others," a seismic impact will be felt. The church ought to be the one community where people come and experience unconditional, selfless love.

The *definition* of love is insufficient without the *deeds* of love. The author of Hebrews encourages the church to "promote love." In some translations it reads, "provoke" love (KJV). One of my favorite translations explains, "and stir up love" (NKJV). We don't usually think of "stirring up love." The Greek word in the original text means to "incite" or to "agitate."

When we use the words *incite* or *agitate* today, they are seldom followed by the word *love*. Modern vernacular will use phrases such as "stirring up trouble" or "stirring up a mess" or even "stirring up a stink." But seldom if ever does one hear about "stirring up love."

Admittedly, I do not do the laundry at our house. My wife would even question if I know the location of the washer and dryer in our home. But I do know that inside of the washing machine there is a bar that moves back and forth. One loads the clothes down into the opening, adds the detergent, and the water begins to fill the machine, and when the prescribed liquid level is reached, that bar in the middle begins to rotate. The name for the bar in the middle of the machine is the "agitator." The agitator's movement is the catalyst to begin the cleaning process. The Bible calls the church to be agitators of love in life. We ought to be the ones moving around this community, stirring up love.

A classic hymn says, "They will know we are Christians by our love." This sentiment is based upon the words of Jesus: "By this all people will know that you are My disciples, if you have love for one another" (John 13:35). The principle is also taught in the Lord's Prayer. I am not referring to the occasion where Jesus taught His disciples "how" to pray, beginning, "Our Father who art in heaven, hallowed be thy name." Rather, I'm referring to an excerpt from His prayer in John 17.

The most passionate prayer of Jesus is found in this chapter. This is an account of Jesus praying: "I pray not only for these, but also for those who believe in Me through their message. May they all be one, as You, Father, are in Me and I am in You. May they also be one in Us, so the world may believe You sent Me" (John 17:20–21). Jesus' prayer was for the church to be so unified that the world would know we are for real. This unity is shown in the way we love one another. I want to be a part of that kind of community!

How does a church build that type of community? Some will mock the attempt, saying, "It can't be done." And the scoffers are correct; the church cannot accomplish this type of community. Fortunately, it is not up to us; Jesus has accomplished it on our behalf. "And I also say to you that you are Peter, and on this rock I will build My church, and the gates of Hades shall not prevail against it" (Matt. 16:18 NKJV). Jesus said, "I *will* build My church." *I will* build My gathering. *I will* build up My believers. God has not called the congregation to do the building. Therefore, we do not need a blueprint. If Jesus has already accomplished this building, then what is God asking the church to do? God is saying, "I don't need you to *build* this community. I need you to *belong* to this community." God is fully capable of building His church. "As for Me, if I am lifted up from the earth I will draw all people to Myself" (John 12:32).

People are longing to belong to community where preference, race, culture, political persuasion, and all other divisive labels no longer hold sway—a community gathered around the centrality of the message of Christ that unites and does not divide. This is the formula for developing a community that matters. A united community can make an impactful difference to all who come in contact.

#withduluth

At First Baptist Church Duluth, we pay serious attention to our presence in the local community. I once heard a seminar speaker challenge, "If your church ceased to exist, would it make any difference in your community?" Our ministry staff is constantly seeking ways to connect the church community with the local community. The result of those efforts is a calendar of over fifty connection events where our church is called upon to actively participate in local efforts. We call this challenge

#withduluth. These events include city government activities, cultural celebrations, benevolence opportunities, service projects, and a wide array of ongoing community ministries.

Being a part of a community is more than purple garbage bags. Community is created when we unite around our common faith to make a noted difference where we live. We long "to be a united community of faith that loves, reaches, and disciples, all people for the Lord Jesus Christ."[10]

CHAPTER THREE

▼ ▼ ▼

Transitioning Friends to Family

The Competence of Multicultural Ministry

*For this reason I kneel before the Father from whom
every family in heaven and on earth is named. I
pray that He may grant you, according to the riches
of His glory, to be strengthened with power in the
inner man through His Spirit. (Ephesians 3:14–16)*

Many people shy away from cross-cultural interactions because
they do not feel competent to develop a relationship across
cultural lines. To avoid these awkward encounters, some choose
to segregate themselves and only spend time with people of a similar background. We are content to do our thing, and to let them
do their thing. For this reason, most churches are monocultural.

But what if a person of another culture became a member of your family? Every family has some branches on the family tree that need explaining. How much more so should the family of God! This family consists of brothers and sisters from every tribe, tongue, and nation; so our churches—our immediate families—should include relationships that don't make sense to the world. The question is: How do we move from accepting people as our friends, to welcoming them as our family?

Some people are willing to befriend a person of another culture, but to make them family may be considered a monumental task. When do friends become family? I'm convinced some people don't understand God's family because they were reared in a dysfunctional family. This may be taboo to talk about and difficult to deal with.

God's Family

I heard about a young couple living in a big city. They went for a night out on the town. The husband arranged for a taxi. When the taxi driver arrived, the couple went to meet their designated transportation. As they got out to the car, the wife turned to the husband and said, "You know, we didn't let the cat out. You need to go back in." As the husband made his way back toward the house door, his wife sat in the backseat of the taxi. She quickly formed an opinion of the driver. He did not, in her eyes, look very reputable. She thought to herself, *I don't want him to think no one is at home,* so she fabricated the reason for her husband having to return to the house. "My husband has gone back in to check on my mother." Soon the husband reappeared from performing his perfunctory duty and exclaimed, "The stupid girl was hiding underneath the bed. I took a coat hanger and tried to get her out. But, it took three or four pokes before I finally got her!"

Family life can be extremely complicated and messy. The apostle Paul mentored a young minister named Timothy. He instructed him on how the church should live like family. "I am writing . . . [so] you will know how to live in the family of God. That family is the church" (1 Tim. 3:15 NCV). One should never think he can love God and not God's family. "The person who loves God must also love other believers" (1 John 4:21 GW).

The Bible refers to the family of God as a body and as a bride. You cannot separate the body from the individual. And you cannot love the person without loving his or her family. In over thirty-five years of pastoring, I have never heard someone say, "Mark, I really love you, but I just cannot stand your bride." Not one time! I am constantly amazed when I hear people say, "I love Christ, but I don't love His church." If you love Christ, you will love His bride. The following are three truths about the family of faith.

A Place of Beginning

The church is referred to as a body and as a bride. The beginning of the body is called *birth*; the beginning for a bride is called a *ceremony*. "For you are all children of God through faith in Christ Jesus" (Gal. 3:26 NLT). We celebrate births by having baby showers, bringing baby gifts, or sending notes of congratulation. This is a time of excitement in the life of any family.

The ceremony of the bride of Christ is baptism. First Peter 3:21 says, "Baptism, which corresponds to this, now saves you (not

the removal of the filth of the flesh, but the pledge of a good conscience toward God) through the resurrection of Jesus Christ."
There are three pictures of baptism in that one verse.

The first picture of baptism is as an *antitype*. The Holman
Christian Standard reads, "Baptism, which corresponds . . ." In
the New King James Version, the translation reads, "Baptism is
an antitype." An antitype is a forerunner. In this instance, it is
an Old Testament picture pointing to a New Testament reality.
Peter has been preaching about Noah. His thought pattern about
the Great Flood, all the water, and the salvation of Noah's family,
drew Peter's attention to the subject of baptism. "By faith Noah
built a ship in the middle of dry land. He was warned about
something he couldn't see, and acted on what he was told. . . . As
a result, Noah became intimate with God" (Heb. 11:7 MSG). Noah
obeyed God. God shut the door of the boat and saved Noah and
his entire family. Baptism is a step of obedience to God that God
will seal you into His family, so that you will live with Him forever and forever.

The second picture of baptism is the *act*. Peter wanted to
clarify if baptism was essential to one's salvation or relationship
with God. The next phrase in 1 Peter 3:21 is in parentheses in
most Bible translations. This parenthetical phrase is actually a
commentary of what has previously been stated. In an attempt to
clarify his position, Peter explained, "not the putting away of the
filth of the flesh . . ." The act of baptism itself is not what saves
people!

I could locate a person on the streets of our city, drag them
inside the church building, take them up the steps to our baptistery location, and immerse them in water; would that individual

be saved? No—they would just be wet! The act of baptism is not what brings about salvation. Baptism has to be more than just the act of getting wet.

The third picture of baptism is as an *answer*. Peter referred to baptism as "the answer of a good conscience toward God." The word *answer* is the word *eperotema* in the Greek language. This is a word to describe a contractual agreement. When one stood before a judge, the judge would ask, "Do you agree to the terms of this contract?" The person would answer and say, "I do." Then the judge would turn to the other party. "Do you also agree to the terms of this contract?" They would answer and say, "I do."

Does this sound familiar? Perhaps your mind has conjured up the picture of a minister standing in front of a bride and groom and asking, "Do you agree?" "I do." "And do you agree?" "I do." I became a pastor at the age of twenty-one. I performed my first wedding ceremony in my first church, the Brown Springs Baptist Church in Mosheim, Tennessee. The couple to be wed was an older couple—a widow and a widower from the congregation. The shy couple shared with me during the wedding planning session, "Pastor, we are so nervous; we will barely be capable of saying anything." I gave the couple an option. "Do you want to repeat vows during your ceremony, or do you just want me to say the vows and ask the two of you to say, 'I do'?"

Feeling relieved of the pressure to perform a recitation in front of guests, the bride responded, "Oh, Pastor, please say the vows, and we will just say, 'I do.'" I further instructed them that I would cue them at the right moment when to say, "I do."

The night of the wedding I began the vows with the groom. I immediately ascertained that he was nervous beyond ability. His eyes were glossed over and were rolling back into his head. He seemed to be ready to pass out. One thing was certain; he was not hearing anything I was saying.

I arrived at the cue and declared, "If so, say, 'I do.'" There was no response—only awkward silence. So I repeated the vows all the way from the beginning and again came to the same point, "If so, say, 'I do.'" Still nothing! I reasoned that surely he would respond upon a third try. So, one more time I yielded the opportunity, "If so, say, 'I do.'" On this attempt his bride took her elbow and punched him in the stomach at the designated time for a response. The groom let out an unintelligible grunt. I hurriedly responded, "I'll take that and let's move on."

Baptism is the way you say, "I do" to Jesus Christ. "I agree with Jesus. I have responded to Jesus. I will act in obedience to Jesus, and I say, 'I do.'" Family is a place of beginnings.

A Place of Belonging

Have you ever felt like you don't belong in your family? Scores of people are searching their family trees today. The website ancestry.com has become a popular pastime for many amateur genealogists searching for their genetic background. I got caught up in this craze for a season and researched my own family tree. I discovered that I am related to an eighteenth-century gentleman named Caesar Rodney, a representative from Delaware to the First Continental Congress and a signer of the Declaration of Independence.

About the time I wanted to stretch out my suspenders and brag about my newly discovered distant relative, I found also a nineteenth-century connection to an outlaw and gunslinger named John Wesley Hardin. Johnny Cash wrote a song about him. He was the son of a Methodist minister, killed forty-two people, and died in prison after serving sixteen years incarcerated. Before I grew too despondent about my close ties to a nefarious killer, I found a twentieth-century tie to actress and humanitarian Audrey Hepburn. We are thirteenth cousins!

Despite these relationships, I will need far more than computer data to feel like I belong with these people. How can one know they belong in the family of faith? The apostle John helps us understand.

> Look at how great a love the Father has given us that we should be called God's children. And we are! The reason the world does not know us is that it didn't know Him. Dear friends, we are God's children now, and what we will be has not yet been revealed. We know that when He appears, we will be like Him because we will see Him as He is. And everyone who has this hope in Him purifies himself just as He is pure. (1 John 3:1–3)

How can one know you belong in the family? You can know you belong in the family because of your objective *position*. The Bible claims that as believers we *are* the children of God. It does not portray this picture as a futuristic promise that one day we will become children of God; nor is it a nebulous, wishful hope. It is the present reality of every believer in Jesus Christ. We are the children of God right now.

John describes the church selected by the Father, and slighted by this world: "What manner of love the Father has bestowed upon us" (1 John 3:1 NKJV). That phrase "what manner of" literally

means, "What country did this come from?" It is an unbelievable
kind of love God the Father has bestowed upon us.

"But God demonstrates His own love toward us, in that
while we were still sinners, Christ died for us" (Rom. 5:8). God
didn't wait for us to get right with Him before He would love us.
He loved us so that we would be right with Him. We have been
selected by the Father. And we have been slighted by the world.

The world didn't recognize Jesus. Why should the world
recognize us? "He was in the world, and the world was created
through Him, yet the world did not recognize Him. He came to
His own, and His own people did not receive Him" (John 1:10–
11). There is a beautiful old spiritual sung at Christmas: "Sweet
Little Jesus Boy . . . we didn't know who you was." So many
people do not recognize the Lord Jesus Christ, and the world does
not recognize us, His followers. We were selected by the Father
and slighted by the world, but now we are God's children. That
position gives us belonging in the family!

You can also know you belong in the family because of your
potential. As the old phrase goes, as a Christian, you are not what
you used to be. You are not what you probably ought to be. But,
praise God you are not yet what you are going to be. God loves
showing off His children. "When Christ, who is our life, shall
appear, then shall ye also appear with him in glory" (Col. 3:4 KJV).
As author Max Lucado puts it, "If God had a refrigerator, your
picture would be on it."[11] God loves you that much!

I was watching the news one evening and a story came
on about a military homecoming. A soldier returned from
Afghanistan. He surprised each of his four daughters during their
school day. In today's modern technology world, people are able

to Skype, message on Facebook, send videos back and forth, and FaceTime, but nothing beats being physically present with one another.

I realize we have the revelation of God's Word, and we have the ability to worship, bringing us close to the Almighty. But one day, we shall be in His very presence, and we shall see Him as He is. When we see Him as He is, we shall become like Him. We know we belong in the family because of our position and our potential.

We know that we belong in the family because of our *purity*. "Everyone who has this hope in Him purifies himself just as He is pure." Note that the word *Him* is capitalized for a reason. The *Him* in this verse is not having the hope in yourself. The *Him* in whom we hope is Jesus Christ. The emphasis is not on merely having hope. The emphasis is on where the hope lies.

People say, "I have my hope in the bank." "I have my hope in the military." "I have my hope in leadership." "I have my hope in the church." The proper place to have your hope is in Him, Jesus Christ. Once one's hope is properly placed, purification takes place. "And everyone who has this hope in Him *purifies* himself" (emphasis mine). There are two words for purity in the Bible. One is the word for absolute purity, and it is always used in reference to God. The second word for purity means to maintain integrity in the face of temptation. This is the word used in the text. The Bible teaches that the only way to be purified is to place our hope firmly in Him.

A Place of Becoming

One of the most famous parables in the Word of God is found in the Gospel of Luke. It is the parable of the prodigal son, and it teaches us that family is a place where we mature. Family is a place where we will make mistakes. There's no greater coming-of-age story found anywhere in all of literature than the story of the prodigal. It teaches us three things about family.

It teaches us that with family, you can experience *forgiveness*. Luke 15:19 reads, "'I am no longer worthy to be called your son. Make me like one of your hired hands.' So he got up and went to his father. But while the son was still a long way off, his father saw him and was filled with compassion. He ran, threw his arms around his neck, and kissed him.'"

Remember the story? The prodigal leaves his father because he thinks he can do better without him. He demands, "Give me what belongs to me." The child who left in verse 12 with a "give me" mentality returns to the father in verse 19 and says, "Make me." That word literally means "mold me" or "shape me." Families forgive you when you have made a mistake.

In His Sermon on the Mount, Jesus taught, "For if you forgive people their wrongdoing, your heavenly Father will forgive you as well" (Matt. 6:14). Church is a place where people ought to be allowed to confess, "I have made a mistake, and I seek forgiveness." Family is where you experience forgiveness.

Family is also a place where you experience *favor*. The story continues with the prodigal coming home to his father. "'Father, I have sinned against heaven and in your sight. I'm no longer worthy to be called your son.' But the father told his slaves, 'Quick! Bring out the best robe and put it on him; put a ring on his finger and sandals on his feet. Then bring the fattened calf and slaughter it, and let's celebrate with a feast'" (Luke 15:21–23).

The homecoming celebration for the prodigal included three gifts. First, the father said, "Put a robe on him." A *robe* was a symbol of righteousness. Then the father said, "Bring here a ring." This would be a family signet ring, a symbol of rule. The signet ring of the family would have identified the bearer as a genuine family member. The final gift from the father was, "Bring him some sandals, some shoes." Shoes were a symbol of relationship. Slaves were not allowed to have shoes. Those who had shoes were family members.

Families celebrate milestones together. Some parents will be awarded stars in their heavenly crowns for the number of times they endured an evening at Chuck E. Cheese. Families celebrate together! We know we are loved and accepted. We experience favor. We enjoy being together.

Families experience forgiveness and favor, and they experience them *forever*. The conclusion of the prodigal story reads, "But we had to celebrate and rejoice, because this brother of yours was dead and is alive again; he was lost and is found" (Luke 15:32). You and I were placed on earth to relate to each other. In over three decades of ministry, I have never observed anyone nearing death ask, "Bring me my diplomas." I have never observed anyone ask, "Bring me the gold watch they gave me on the day of my retirement." I've never observed anyone ask, "Please let me see my trophies one last time."

I have, however, sat with dear Christian brothers and sisters who pleaded with me, "Gather my family. Bring me my family." Family is forever! I am aware that some people have a demented view of family because of a dysfunctional upbringing. When I preach on this subject, some people usually challenge me because of their difficult background. I have to explain to them that God's family is different—better—than our families. When you become a part of God's family, you have a Father who loves you unconditionally and wants you to learn how to love each other similarly. The family of faith will always be your family.

I have always admired George H. W. Bush (the elder Bush). He may be my favorite president. In an interview, the former president was once asked, "What's your greatest accomplishment?" This man may be the most accomplished person of my lifetime. He was a fighter pilot in World War II, United States ambassador to China, vice president of the United States for eight years, and eventually president for four years, winning victory in the Persian Gulf War. He is the father of two governors and one of them became president.

What did this man with such a rich résumé of achievements reveal as his most valuable contribution? "My greatest accomplishment in life and what I would like for someone to say at my funeral service is . . . my children still want to come home."[12] That is a beautiful picture of family—a place to come home. Family is a place of becoming, a place of belonging, and a place of beginnings. Family gives forgiveness and favor, and family is forever.

Moving from Friends to Family

At First Baptist Church Duluth, we have devised a plan for transitioning friends to family across cultural barriers. We call this process "Cross Class." Cross Class is a cross-cultural, cross-generational gathering at the cross of Jesus Christ. I had observed people struggling to find a place of belonging and unable to cross cultural barriers to find a faith family. Due to this perceived lack, in 2014, I began a study in my home to examine ways to develop cross-cultural competence. The original group had twelve families from six different countries participate.

I secured a new curriculum from authors Mark DeYmaz and Oneya Fennell Okuwobi entitled, *The Multi-Ethnic Christian Life Primer: A Guide to Walking, Working, and Worshipping Together as One.* This eight-week study was in the pre-publication stage at the time. With the authors' permission, we became one of the first churches to utilize the material. This gathering provided robust discussion and began a cascade of ideas for methods to open our congregation to diversity.

At the conclusion of the beta group's study, I challenged the original team to divide and multiply. The goal was to team up two families of different ethnic origin to be the catalyst for the formation of a new home group. From the original group, five groups were formed. The criteria for each newly formed group was to be comprised of at least three ethnic groups, and to have at least a thirty-year age span between the oldest the youngest group members. This would assure that every group be identifiably multicultural and experientially multigenerational. To date, there have been a total of seven groups complete the study, amassing over seventy-five church members trained in a cross-cultural lifestyle, representing thirteen different countries.

The concept of cross-cultural competence is an ongoing goal for the multicultural church. The education process is never a completed task. The graduates of this study never want the course to end. Friendships are formulated that have been exemplary for the entire congregation. By sitting in a living room, discussing cultural differences, and opening up to new thoughts and ideas, we are transitioning friends into authentic family.

CHAPTER FOUR

▼ ▼ ▼

Anyone Headed My Way?

The Charge of Multicultural Ministry

Can two walk together without agree-
ing to meet? (Amos 3:3)

Who is going where we are going? Who is headed in the same direction we are headed? Every church must answer these questions. God never intended for us to do this Christian life alone. He intended for us to do it in family. Finding family to share the load is a biblical and superior way to travel through life.

A principle I learned from Henry Blackaby's *Experiencing God* study is to find where God is at work and join Him there. With that principle in mind, First Baptist Church Duluth has developed a strategy to create partnerships that help us accomplish our mission. There are a variety of ways in which we partner with those who are outside of our fellowship in order to accomplish the mission of our church.

One of those is the Cooperative Program. The Cooperative Program is a network of more than forty thousand Southern Baptist churches giving a percentage of their income to a united mission fund for the support of mission efforts at home and around the world. Despite challenging financial times both locally and nationally, our church has increased our percentage of gifts to this historic mission offering every year for the past six years!

The Cooperative Program supports more than four thousand missionaries internationally. It supports five-thousand-plus missionaries in North America. It supports six Southern Baptist seminaries that are training the next generation of Christian leaders. It supports our Georgia Baptist Mission Board and its church-planting efforts. We belong to a convention of Baptist churches who collectively support the largest missionary movement in the history of Christianity. This is a great partnership.

Second, we partner with the North American Mission Board of the Southern Baptist Convention. First Baptist Church Duluth is one of the first "Sending" churches signing up to aid in the effort to plant churches in "Send Cities." These Send Cities are the thirty mega-cities in America with the largest percentage of lost people. First Baptist Church of Duluth has adopted the city of Atlanta and is sponsoring two church planters in the metro area. In addition to our home area, FBC Duluth is instrumental in the development of a church plant in our sister city of Duluth, Minnesota.

First Baptist Church Duluth had been a partner with the International Mission Board of the Southern Baptist Convention for over a century. Fifty percent of our Great Commission

Missions Offering (received throughout the year) is forwarded to the IMB to support global mission efforts of Southern Baptists. This offering has increased four of the last five years and has set new records for missions' contributions from the FBCD family.

Another strategic partnership for our church was becoming an affiliate member of the Mosaix Global Network, an interdenominational movement promoting multiethnic churches throughout America. Early in the development of strategy toward multicultural goals, we took our entire staff to an annual retreat scheduled by the leadership board of Mosaix. This was an introduction for our church into the path of multicultural ministry and a great beginning point of networking to find practitioners who could help us find answers to our multitude of puzzling questions along this path.

Determining a Direction

What are the criteria for determining who the church will partner with? The missions efforts of many churches are almost like throwing a dart at a world map and saying, "Let's go there." There must be some biblical insights into how a church establishes direction! And how can the church accomplish going without initiating partnerships? Here are three mandates for partnership from Amos 3:3.

The Accord of Partnerships

"Can two walk together . . ." The phrase "walk together" literally means to be joined together. It's a picture word likened to a three-legged race one has at a picnic, physically joined together.

"Can two walk together unless they agree to meet?" In parts of England, it is customary to announce a wedding engagement by saying, "Jim and Jane are walking out together." The whole idea is that they have become one. They have joined themselves together.

Prior to walking together, there need be four agreements. First of all, the two parties need to be *moved from a shared place.* "Can two walk together unless they agree to meet?" There has to be a designated place for the two to meet. The partnership requires a beginning point. There has to be a merger at some point.

When I first moved to Georgia I noticed there is a Waffle House restaurant about every 150 yards here. One morning I had a scheduled breakfast meeting at a Waffle House. Unfortunately, I was at the Waffle House on Old Peachtree Road and Interstate 85, and the person I was meeting was at the Waffle House at Highway 120 and Interstate 85, approximately three miles apart. Thirty minutes after our appointed meeting time, I realized, *I am not at the right place.* Can two walk together unless they agree as to where they are supposed to meet? The two need a shared starting place.

Not only are they moved from a shared place, they are *modified by a shared pace.* My wife Glenda's walking pace is a slow jog for me. She will occasionally ask me to take an evening walk with her around the neighborhood. I will ask, "Now, are we walking, or are we jogging?" She always responds, "I am just going for a walk." I have learned to be a little more inquisitive: "What kind of shoes are you wearing?" If Glenda says, "I'm wearing tennis shoes," I know to prepare for a workout ending with some wind sprints. Can two walk together unless they share the same pace?

One cannot lag behind or step ahead. You are walking together in pace with one another.

Third, two cannot walk together unless they are *motivated by a shared purpose.* Moving in the same direction involves having the same ultimate goal and arriving at the same location. If someone says, "I'm headed toward Downtown Atlanta," and someone else says, "I'm headed toward Downtown Atlanta," and the third person says, "I'm headed toward Downtown Atlanta," it would be a wise choice of resources to combine efforts and take the same vehicle for all three. Not only will this save resources, it will also provide companionship for the journey. There is an obvious shared purpose when people are moving in the same direction. Another benefit is to encourage one another. We will all rejoice when we arrive at the destination.

A final agreement necessary to walk together is to be *mobilized by a shared price.* The best way to accomplish a big goal is to do it one step at a time. The old adage is, "The best way to eat an elephant is one bite at a time." The question is, *Are you willing to accept your bite in this endeavor?* This final step of agreement involves personal investment of time, energy, and financial resources. Because many are unwilling to make a genuine commitment, this is where partnerships are severed.

All four of these principles are true of our partnership with Jesus Christ. You have to meet Jesus at a mutually agreed-upon *place* before you can become a follower of Christ. The Bible clearly instructs everyone to meet Jesus at the cross. There is no other way! Jesus said, "I am the way, the truth, and the life. No one comes to the Father except through Me" (John 14:6). The cross is the starting point for the Christian life.

Having met Jesus at the cross, one is commanded to keep *pace* with Him by following Him in truth and in spirit. The Christian life now has a newfound sense of direction to it, a pursuit of a heavenly calling, and a new divine *purpose*. Jesus paid everything required for my salvation upon the cross, but He also commands us to pay a price in service: "Take up [your] cross and follow Me" (Matt. 16:24).

The Advantages of Partnerships

Two are better than one because they have a good reward for their efforts. For if either falls, his companion can lift him up; but pity the one who falls without another to lift him up. Also, if two lie down together, they can keep warm; but how can one person alone keep warm? And if someone overpowers one person, two can resist him. A cord of three strands is not easily broken. (Eccl. 4:9–12)

There are three advantages in having significant partnerships. The first advantage is that partnerships create *a better success*. Verse 9 points out, "Two are better than one because they have a good reward for their efforts." Have you ever heard the phrase, "Two heads are better than one"? This common colloquialism is actually an Old English proverb attributed to a poet named John Heywood in 1546. However, the principle goes all the way back to the Old Testament. It is always better to have a second opinion. There is a better success rate when two or more are involved.

The second advantage of strategic partnerships is *better security*. The Life Alert company has made a fortune by using a phrase that touches on the security issues of every senior adult, "I've fallen, and I can't get up." The wisdom of Ecclesiastes addressed this concern centuries earlier. There is a secure feeling in knowing that someone is there if I fall and I am going to be picked up. Someone is specifically watching out for me. Possibly you have been a caregiver for someone who has a risk of falling. Or maybe you have helped someone during their time of deepest and darkest need. Partnerships provided needed security.

Ecclesiastes paints the picture of a cold winter night, when it is good to have someone to snuggle up next to and help keep you warm. Before there were heaters, there was always an opportunity to snuggle up to the one you love. It is a wonderful feeling of security to know that someone will aid me in the coldest, darkest moments of my life.

The third advantage of partnerships is *better strength*. "A cord of three strands is not easily broken." Have you heard the phrase, "I've got your back"? Someone is standing up for you. No matter what the world may throw into your path, a true partner will protect you. Enemies seldom attack from the front. In an attempt to surprise and overcome, attacks are typically when you least expect them. But a true partner will be watching out on your behalf. Partnerships provide the advantage of better success, better security, and better strength.

Appreciation for Partnerships

The apostle Paul was a missionary who had loving partners taking care of his needs.

> I give thanks to my God for every remembrance of you, always praying with joy for all of you in my every prayer, because of your partnership in the gospel from the first

day until now. . . . It is right for me to think this way about all of you, because I have you in my heart, and you are all partners with me in grace, both in my imprisonment and in the defense and establishment of the gospel. (Phil. 1:3–5, 7)

Paul was thanking the Philippian church for their partnership. In some translations, the word *fellowship* is used. This is a very interesting word. In the original language, it is the opposite of the word for *friction*. What is friction? Friction is caused when two objects are headed in the opposite direction, or when one object is moving and the other is stationary. But when two objects are headed in the same direction at the same pace, there is no friction. This is fellowship. This is partnership! Paul was praising God that he and the Philippians were not headed in the opposite direction. Likewise, I am praising God for ministry partners that are neither moving in an opposite direction, nor sitting stationary.

After Paul praised the Philippian church for their partnership, he offered to pray for them. Genuine partners pray for one another and encourage one another. They lift each other up. Paul prays three things for them in verses 9–11. The first is in verse 9: "And I pray this: that your love will keep on growing in knowledge and every kind of discernment." He prayed for the Philippians to be *saturated in devotion*. Paul wanted them to continue to grow spiritually. The phrase "to keep on growing" is a building term related to how a mason would lay bricks together in the building of a wall. Paul wanted to see layer after layer after layer of growth in the Philippian believers.

Paul indicates two measures of the depth of love: the depth of knowledge and the depth of discernment. The word for *knowledge* is a word indicating personal knowledge. It is a word depicting experiential knowledge, not academia. Paul was a scholar and I am sure a great proponent of academic achievement at the highest level. Yet, he is praying here for church members to experience living truth in such a way that they can spiritually discern it. The word *discernment* is a unique word found only here in all of the New Testament, a word that communicates moral insight. Paul was challenging the Philippians: "I want you to have the knowledge that comes with experience, and I want you to have moral insight into this world."

The second thing Paul prayed for the Philippians was that they might be *sound in doctrine.* In verse 10, Paul continues: "So that you can approve the things that are superior." The word "approve" literally means to put to the test. Paul was challenging the Philippian believers to put God's Word to the test and see that He is truthful!

Dr. John Phillips, in his commentary on the book of Philippians, says, "The enemy of the best is good. Unfortunately, there are many good people. We hear, 'He is good. She is good.' There are many good ideas, but the enemy of the best is good."[13] My first pastorate was in a small town in Tennessee. I served the Brown Springs Baptist Church in Mosheim. One of the key leaders in the church was a retired banker named Mr. Wisecarver. I pastored this church in the early '80s, and Mr. Wisecarver had been in the community since the turn of the twentieth century. He had led the local community bank through the Great Depression. Mr. Wisecarver knew literally every family in the community and he knew their family history and pedigree.

When I talked to the stately former executive about certain folks in the community, he would often respond, "Yes, yes. Good citizen. Good citizen." This positive evaluation meant the individual paid their taxes and had never been in trouble with the law. This surface reading told me something useful about people, but was useless in ascertaining spiritual health. The enemy of the best often is good.

Paul told the Philippians of his prayers for them to prove what is superior because we have a perfect Word from a perfect God. The church does not have something "good" to offer this world. We have some*one* superior to offer this world. Paul prayed for them to give up that which is good for that which is best so to make a real difference and have maximum impact.

Paul prayed for the Philippians to be saturated in devotion and sound in doctrine. The third part of Paul's prayer was for the Philippians to be *sincere in their deeds.* The last part of verse 10 and 11 reads, ". . . and can be pure and blameless in the day of Christ, filled with the fruit of righteousness that comes through Jesus Christ to the glory and praise of God."

Some versions use the word *sincere* here in place of *pure.* The Greek word used here literally refers to making a judgment in the sunlight. This is a wonderfully rich picture of early New Testament life. In the first century, a potter would sometimes find imperfection—cracks—in his work. Not wanting to discard hours of toil and labor, he would fill the cracks with wax and then paint over them. The potter would sell the vessel as new, all the while knowing it was cracked. Having been a pastor for over thirty-five years, I know that churches are filled with insincere, cracked vessels.

Reputable dealers would put a label on their pottery reading, *"Sinceria,"* which meant, "Hold it up to the light." The dealer was being honest. This has been made new. It has been made perfect and fully functional. This vessel has been made right. Every single Sunday at FBC Duluth a congregation filled with formerly cracked pots gathers to hear a message from their formerly cracked-pot preacher. But, we have been made new, and we have been made right. Hold us up to the light of the Son of God because He is the one who has made us perfect. I am sincerely pure because of my relationship with Jesus Christ.

Paul's criterion for determining sincerity is an individual's fruit (v. 11). An insincere Christian produces insincere fruit, bad fruit, or no fruit. If you are an insincere vessel covered in wax, then you will produce nothing more than wax fruit. Wax fruit is aesthetically appealing to the eye. It makes for a wonderful decoration, but it provides no nutritional value.

Sincere Christians produce sincere fruit. That's why Jesus said in John 15:4–5, "Remain in Me, and I in you. Just as a branch is unable to produce fruit by itself unless it remains on the vine, so neither can you unless you remain in Me. I am the vine; you are the branches. The one who remains in Me and I in him produces much fruit." If I am in a relationship with Jesus and partnered with Him, I will produce real fruit. The question of introspection is, "Are you real?" Are you producing real fruit because of your partnership with Jesus Christ, or are you merely dressing up to look nice to the world? It's never a bad idea to check the fruit in your life and make sure you are abiding in the Vine. A genuine partnership produces real fruit.

Paul said, "I appreciate you and your partnership. I appreciate what you have stood for when you have stood by me. I am praying that you will be saturated in your devotion and that you will be sound in your doctrine. I'm praying that you will be sincere in your deeds." These criteria for partnership have shaped the way we do missions at First Baptist Church. Consider the following four stories of church-planting partnerships established during the past five years.

I Have a Brother (India)

Prior to my arrival at Duluth, I served as a trustee for LifeWay Christian Resources, the publishing arm of the Southern Baptist Convention. In my last year as a trustee I served as a committee chair and as the secretary to the board. The committee that I chaired was responsible for employee mission trips. At the time, LifeWay promoted mission efforts by providing time off with pay and scholarship for half of mission trip costs through the company. I was encouraged as a board member to consider going with the employees on one of their 2010 trips. Prayerfully looking at the 2010 schedule, I chose to join the team to India in February of that year.

While preparing, I was contacted by the Pastor Search Team of First Baptist Church Duluth. Early in the discussion process I shared with the team my commitment to being on mission in India. They graciously scheduled around my previous commitment. I resigned my position in Indianapolis, served my last Sunday in the first week of February, moved our belongings to interim housing in Duluth on the following week, and left for two weeks in India with the LifeWay team. Upon my return, I preached my first service at my new ministry post in Duluth on the first of March. I often tell people that I moved to Duluth from India, which is technically correct.

The LifeWay trip to India was coordinated by a mission organization called *International Commission*. This group, based in Lewisville, Texas, creates partnerships between American churches and international ministries for the purposes of evangelism and church planting. I had thought that my experience in India was in all probability a once-in-a-lifetime experience. Little did I realize the preparation God was doing in my heart.

On my first day at FBC Duluth, I met two Indian families: Newton and Shruiti Reuben Samuel, and Noble and Ruth Udaikar Daniel. Both were elated to hear of my recent journey to their homeland. (Note: Newton Samuel and Noble Daniel have both been ordained as deacon leaders at FBCD. Noble is serving as vice-chairman of the deacon body at the time of this writing.) I had been informed of the rapid changes that were happening demographically in the community of Duluth. However, I did not know that South Asian people were one of the fastest growing people groups in our area. The Indian population has grown to such an extent that a large Hindu temple has moved in as one of the nearest neighbors to our church facilities—within a few hundred yards of the church entrance.

I began to consider the obvious timing of my new passion for the nation of India and an effective ministry organization to aid us in establishing international partners. For the next two years, FBC Duluth worked with International Commission to plant churches in the city of Kakinada, a city in the Southeast Indian state of Andhra Pradesh. This partnership with a church-planting movement in the area yielded dozens of new church plants.

Regular missionary journeys to India opened the eyes of church members to their neighbors who call that region home. People began sharing with me of encounters in the grocery store, or the bank, or a mail carrier. FBCD members often asked, "Where are you from?" If the person responded, "India," the immediate response was, "Our church goes to India often!" This church-planting effort opened doors of interaction and provided natural conversation starters.

During my first year as pastor of FBCD, the chairman of deacons was a retired International Mission Board missionary, Tom Jones. Tom and his wife, Nancy, had served for over two decades in Nairobi, Kenya. Early in my tenure as pastor, Tom informed me that their daughter, Sara, and her husband, John Davenport, were currently serving the IMB as missionaries in Delhi, India. The Jones family were excited that their children were coming home for the Christmas holiday and they wanted me to meet their missionary family members. I was later informed that the Davenports were bringing with them a pastor from the Delhi area, an Indian national, Pastor Daniel Kumar. John wanted me to meet Pastor Daniel and to learn of his vision to place a church-planting catalyst in every city in northern India with more than one million residents.

I was delighted to meet John and Sara and hear about their missionary calling to India. And I sat in amazement to hear from their friend Daniel Kumar, pastor of the Good News Centre in Delhi, as he articulated a plan to establish a church-planting movement in what he termed the "gateway cities" of India. Pastor

Daniel had identified twenty-six such cities and was currently working in five of them. This plan was exhilarating, and in the areas currently operational, it was working extremely effectively. I told Pastor Daniel and the Davenports of my dream to have a mutually beneficial partnership in which we would assist in church planting and simultaneously learn cultural nuances that would make us more effective to be clear witnesses in our local context.

Pastor Daniel perked up in interest of our church's desire to reach South Asian people in our local area. Daniel said, "I have a brother who lives here." I responded, "Do you mean in the States (USA)?" His response blew me away. "I mean here in Duluth! His name is Kadmiel and he and his wife, Isoleth, are struggling to find a church they sense has a heart for internationals." I pleaded for the opportunity to meet his relatives and enlist his brother as a personal cultural consultant to educate me in South Asian ministry. During Daniel's visit to our area, he arranged my first meeting with his brother Kadmiel.

For the next year, Kadmiel and I met periodically to discuss ministry ideas and plan outreach events to impact the Indian portion of our community. I wanted to clearly portray my motivation in pursuing this partnership, so I never asked Kadmiel to join our church as a member. He and his family had been attending another evangelical church in the area. Our relationship was a mutual desire to make a Kingdom influence on the South Asian community. At the end of that first year, Kadmiel came to me and shared his desire for himself and his family to become a part of the First Baptist Church Duluth ministry.[14]

Since establishing an ongoing partnership with the Good News Centre in Delhi and Pastor Daniel Kumar, FBC Duluth has adopted and now sponsors the church-planting catalyst in two of the twenty-six gateway cities—Amritsar and Bhopal. I have had the privilege of leading a pastor's preview trip to India for the purposes of education and motivation. Soliciting additional ministry partners is an ongoing ministry task.

Pastor Daniel returns to the States to visit his brother Kadmiel and gives an annual report to FBCD. Our 2014 team to India included Lindsay Lapole, recently retired Southern Territory Planned Giving Director for the Salvation Army. Pastor Daniel shared with Lindsay the enormous vision that God has placed upon his heart. Lindsay, upon return from the mission trip, immediately made plans to draw grant proposals to solicit funding sources and secure additional partners. In 2015, First Baptist Church Duluth was awarded a $100,000 grant from the Georgia Baptist Health Care Foundation for the purpose of establishing a medical missionary bus for the state of Orissa, the poorest and most persecuted state in all of India. This medical missionary bus is now fully staffed and completely operational.

The providence of God had taken a pastor—ME—having just returned from a missionary journey to India, and placed me in a church surrounded by a rapidly growing Indian population. I would serve alongside a retired IMB missionary as deacon chairman, who has a daughter and son-in-law currently serving as missionaries to Delhi. The missionaries to Delhi have an Indian national pastor friend with a vision to plant churches in his homeland, and the pastor has a brother who is a near neighbor to the church facilities in Duluth. The brother's family is looking for an internationally minded local ministry. This is the supreme example of being headed in the same direction!

That's Where I'm From (Mexico)

The strategy was to plant churches in the homeland of the largest unreached people groups in our local area. After beginning with church planting efforts in India, our attention turned toward Mexico. Gwinnett County, where FBCD in located, is home to the largest Hispanic population in the state of Georgia. Although there is extreme diversity among the Spanish speakers—some are from Central America and others are from South America—the largest single group is Mexican Americans.

In seeking sources to aid us in these efforts, I learned that our state Baptist convention had an ongoing partnership with Mexico and the Yucatan Peninsula. This area is most noted for the resort city of Cancun. But outside of the tourist area is extreme poverty and genuine need for church planting partners. FBC Duluth partnered with the Georgia Baptist Convention and aided church planters in the small villages of Solferino and Tres Reyes. Trips to Solferino culminated in digging a well as a water source for the city and building a first-phase church building at the well location. Prior to the well's completion, village residents walked five miles through jungle territory to retrieve drinking water. Now, the place where one comes to collect drinking water also offers the "living water" of the gospel!

Unfortunately, due to budget restraints, the Georgia Baptist Convention discontinued the Yucatan partnership. Key contacts that were instrumental in continuing our work in the area were brought home to the States. I sought the help of our International Mission Board, asking if they had any similar church-planting opportunities for us to partner with. Upon initial contact with the IMB, I learned that the missionary coordinator for such work was a Facebook friend of mine from my days in Indiana named Rich Fleming. Rich immediately asked me to consider the possibility of adopting the Bajio region of Mexico for our next church-planting endeavor.

Bajio is a five-state region in north central Mexico. When I received the potential new assignment, I researched the area. At the time, our church was conducting a Tuesday evening Bible study for Spanish speakers in the home of one of our members. I dropped in on the weekly study armed with maps and information about the potential new area of ministry. When I put the map of the region on my computer screen, one of our Spanish speakers gave a shout of elation: "That's where I'm from!" He pointed in the middle of the map to the state of San Luis Potosi (the name of the state and also the name of the capital city—much like New York, New York). Felipe Vega and his family are probably the longest-attending Spanish speakers in our congregation. Now, we were considering going to his hometown to plant churches!

Soon afterward I contacted missionary Rich Fleming to tell him we would like to adopt the city of San Luis Potosi in the Bajio region. Rich reluctantly informed me that there were currently no IMB personnel in that state. He assured me of the safety of the region, but any ongoing partnership would need to be forged with local nationals and would necessitate crossing the language barrier. San Luis Potosi is a city of over one and a half million people with less than 1 percent identifying as evangelical Christians and only four existing Baptist churches.

Local church leaders in San Luis were thrilled to learn of our interest in establishing a church-planting partnership. A vision trip was planned for the fall of 2014. On that trip, I met Pastor Florian Vazquez of the Iglesia Bautista Emanuel de San Luis (Emanuel Baptist Church). Emanuel is the one of the oldest and most established Baptist churches in the city, and Pastor Florian has pastored the church for over twenty years. In the midst of the planning stages, Rich Fleming contacted me to share good news: the IMB was moving a couple to San Luis Potosi to solidify the work in that area. Tommy and Donna Beard were veteran IMB personnel in Mexico relocating to the San Luis area for their new assignment at the beginning of 2015.

First Baptist Church Duluth immediately became partners with a national church planter, Josue Antonio Arellano. This dynamic young man came from the Emanuel church and was planting a new church named Iglesia Bautista Vida Nueva (New Life Baptist Church). In less than a year, the new congregation has grown to the point of constituting its own church and is now seeking ways to partner with us in reproducing additional evangelical work in the area. God provided us an outstanding interpreter for our work. Jerry Agullar, a local church leader in the Emanuel church, has outstanding English skills and he, too, wants to become a church planter in the San Luis area.

Felipe Vega and his family, natives of the San Luis area and FBCD members, have made multiple trips with our church to the San Luis mission field. God provided through a willing voice of obedience a missionary partnership that has already assisted in one church plant and is seeking many more in this needed area. The International Mission Board, local Mexican Baptist leadership, and First Baptist Church Duluth are all headed in the same direction!

Pastor, That's Our Language (Nigeria)

On Palm Sunday 2015, First Baptist Church Duluth celebrated with an outdoor baptism service. We borrowed a portable baptistery and on a beautiful, sunny afternoon we gathered on the church parking lot to portray to our neighbors and to the world our faith. One of the baptism candidates was a new believer in our congregation from the nation of Nigeria, Abbie Abujowole. Abbie and her two children were the fourth Nigerian family to come to FBC Duluth within a year.

I had been praying for months for God to give me a clear direction as to where our next church planting energies should be spent. After four Nigerian families had come to our church, I felt this could possibly be the answer to my prayer. I shared my sense of spiritual direction with our church missions committee. The first reaction was one of extreme caution. Nigeria is a nation where believers face severe persecution. Moreover, I had no missionary contacts to aid in the formation of such a partnership.

No plans were being made—only prayers that God would provide the way in His timing. Later that year, I was browsing my Facebook page and learned that a pastor friend of mine from my days in Indiana was relocating to the county adjacent to me. Dr. David Pope and I had served in numerous state convention leadership committees. For him to be coming as a near neighbor was exciting news. I messaged him immediately and shared that we would need to get together for a meal and catch up on each other's lives. I didn't hear a response from David for a couple of weeks. Then a response came with an apology: "Sorry for the delay. I have been in *Nigeria*. Would you like to get together for lunch soon?" I sat in absolute amazement for a moment, and then responded. "David, I think you are the answer to months of prayer. Yes, we need to do lunch real soon!"

That lunch meeting was a combination reunion and revival meeting. It was a joy to learn how God was using my friend David and his wife, Cindy. Since our days together in Indiana, they had been appointed IMB missionaries to Burkina Faso in West Africa. After two years on the mission field, they had returned to the States to be near family. Now David was serving as the vice president of a ministry called *Reach the Rest*. This parachurch organization is designed to link American churches with national leaders in the hardest-to-reach areas of the world. David was using his contacts from his days in West Africa to offer leadership in that area of the world. He had just returned from his journey to Nigeria with the hope of finding a partner church to adopt a church-planting movement among Yoruba-speaking Muslims in the area outside the city of Ibadan.

I asked David if he and Cindy would come and explain the ministry at a dinner meeting in our home. I invited all four of the new Nigerian families to come to this meeting. And I also included the families from other African nations involved in our congregation: Ghana, Cameroon, Liberia, and Ethiopia. David and Cindy shared about the three primary language groups in Nigeria: Hausa, Igbo, and Yoruba. Each has its own unique culture. The Hausa are predominantly in the northern half of the country and are almost exclusively Muslim. The Igbo are in the Southwest corner of Nigeria and make up about 20 percent of the nation's population. The Igbo are almost evenly split among Muslims and Christians. Roman Catholicism has a very strong influence among the Igbo people. The Yoruba are predominantly in the Southeast corner of Nigeria. This is the most heavily populated area of the nation and until recently has been marked by strong evangelical Christian influence. Due to the migration of Muslims from the North, there is a substantial population of Yoruba-speaking Muslims in the region.

As David shared about his dream of establishing evangelical churches among the Yoruba-speaking Muslims, one of our church members, Bab, stood and said, "Pastor, that is our language. We will help you plant this church."[15] At the end of the dinner meeting we joined together in prayer for the next steps in becoming a church-planting catalyst in Nigeria. In August of 2015, I journeyed to Nigeria to learn how we could potentially aid in the work. I affectionately refer to this trip as my trip to Africa with the Pope (Dr. David Pope).

While on this trip I met Reach the Rest President Mike Jackson and their field coordinator in Nigeria, James Olarinre. Dr. Pope and James took me into the bush country to meet the person with whom our church would partner. The journey was about an hour trip outside the major city of Ibadan down a one-lane dirt road to a tiny village called Fada. There I met Samuel Ojewole. This former public school science teacher had left his home to establish a church in this tiny village and was training eleven leaders from nearby villages on how to replicate his success in carrying the gospel to this gospel-quenched area. The Ojewoles live in a one-room, mud-thatched home, and have taken in a dozen children discarded by Muslim families because of their conversion to Christianity. Our church has begun a partnership with Samuel Ojewole and his church-planting school because we believe that we are most definitely headed in the same direction.

You Will Have Touched Half the World (China)

Upon return from FBC's first missionary journey to India, we conducted a celebration service. At the end of each service we extend a "meet the pastor" time for all first-time guests. That Sunday, a Chinese gentleman waited patiently to introduce himself to me. "My name is John Cao and I am a missionary to China," said the articulate visitor. "I am very impressed by your work in India. You need to do the same in China. If you influence the nations of India and China, you will have touched half the world!"

My first reaction was that my new acquaintance was being pithy and witty. However, I soon learned that his challenge was intended to be very serious. John works with an organization called Mainland China Mission International. He spends six months in China each year and six months in the state of North Carolina, where his wife and family reside. I asked how a missionary to China that resides in North Carolina found his way to be in a service in Duluth, Georgia, on a Sunday when we were talking about church-planting efforts in India. John shared that he had recently purchased a home in the neighborhood across the street from our church. The original purpose of the house was to be a retirement home for his mother. She had selected the area due to having Chinese friends in the local area. However, John's mother changed her mind and returned to China. So John decided to use the house as a ministry asset.

John articulated his vision of rotating underground church pastors from China to the United States for some time of respite and safety removed from the public eye. The missionary asked if our church would consider "caring for" these pastors by providing services acclimating immigrants to a new land. Most of these pastors and their families would have limited English skills and would need to rely heavily on aid from the church for basic activities. Over the past five years we have welcomed Pastor Jack, Pastor Mark, and Pastor Su, and their families into our congregation (American names protecting their identity).

John has introduced me to Mainland China Mission International President, Dr. Samuel Fang. His offices are in Washington, Pennsylvania. Dr. Fang is seeking ways to broaden and deepen our partnership, including provision of Mandarin interpretation at our worship services. Mandarin is the fourth largest language group in the Duluth area (behind English, Spanish, and Korean). Dr. Fang is planning a vision trip for FBCD in 2017 to see the multifaceted ministries of their organization's church-planting efforts, pastor-training schools, orphanages, adoption agency, and soon-to-come senior adult living ministries. A Chinese missionary happened into a Baptist church in Georgia and found they were both headed in the same direction!

Providence and Partnership

Time and time again over the past five years God has placed strategic partners in our path that are obviously headed in the same direction as First Baptist Church Duluth. Learning to recognize these divine encounters and accentuating these opportunities has been a tremendous testimony of the sovereignty of God. For readers contemplating taking this journey to multicultural ministry, here is a word of advice: open yourself up to the possibilities of partnerships that allow free exchange of information with a mutual desire to reach the nations in your church field. The sovereignty of God is a major theme in telling the First Baptist story. I believe with all my heart that God will provide the people as well as the financial resources necessary to complete His work. The leader pursuing multicultural ministry needs to constantly be observing God's directional and provisional will so as to seize the opportunities placed in his path.

CHAPTER FIVE

▼ ▼ ▼

Stick Your Head out the Window

The Climate of Multicultural Ministry

*From the Issacharites, who understood the times and
knew what Israel should do. (1 Chronicles 12:32)*

During World War II, baseball announcers were not allowed to give a weather report from the ballpark. Military heads believed releasing atmospheric information could potentially aid the enemy if bombers were planning a flyover. Therefore, announcers would avoid saying it was a fair and sunny day or a cloudy day or even a rainy day. St. Louis Cardinals Hall-of-Famer Dizzy Dean went on to become the ball club's announcer. During a gameday broadcast, Dean tried to fill airtime during an obvious rain delay in the action. The former baseball hero was quickly running out of stories to fill the airtime when he suddenly blurted out, "If you folks don't know what's holding up this game, just stick your head out the window!"

Sometimes the answer to a question is painfully obvious. But people have a tendency to miss the obvious.

The Pharisees and Sadducees approached, and as a test, asked Him to show them a sign from heaven. He answered them: "When evening comes you say, 'It will be good weather because the sky is red.' And in the morning, 'Today will be stormy because the sky is red and threatening.' You know how to read the appearance of the sky, but you can't read the signs of the times." (Matt. 16:1–3)

Jesus challenged first-century spiritual leaders for not being capable of reading the signs of the times. Today, leaders do not understand what is deterring the Church because we are not sticking our head out the window and reading the signs of the times.

A Native American reservation elected a new chief to lead their tribe. A group approached their new leader with confidence and asked him, "This winter . . . will it be cold?" The chief looked to the sky and pronounced his prognostication: "Yes. Winter will be very cold this year. Store up wood." The new leader secretly embraced many aspects of modern technology not popular among all the tribesmen. Desiring to make a good impression with his first act as leader, the chief called the National Weather Service to confirm his bold prediction. A disembodied voice at the National Weather Service Hotline confirmed his speculation, "Yes, we are predicting a cold winter."

The fall season arrived with warm, beautiful days, causing some of the tribe to question the predictive ability of their new chief. After several successive days of unseasonably warm temperatures, a group questioned their leader. "Chief," they asked, "are you sure it's going to be cold this winter?" He once again looked to the sky and said, "It will be cold this winter. Store up wood." Again, he phoned the National Weather Service and was reassured, "Yes, it's going to be *very* cold this winter."

Fall was turning into the early days of winter, yet the climate was hotter and hotter. It was becoming increasingly difficult to stand by the new chief's original proclamation. The tribe wanted to give their leader an opportunity to recant. Therefore, they asked him a third time, "Chief, are you certain it's going to be cold this winter?" He looked to the sky, and said, "It is going to be cold this winter. Store up wood."

He placed a call to the National Weather Service for a third time, and asked again, "Are you sure it is going to be cold this winter?" The National Weather Service said, "Yes, it is going to be *bitterly* cold this winter." The chief was perplexed as to how the government agency could be so assured in the midst of such seemingly overwhelming evidence to the contrary. He pleaded for some clarity: "How can you be so certain?" The weather service employee calmly explained, "Have you seen how much wood they are storing up at the reservation?"

Reading the Signs of the Times

Many people misread the signs of the times. One thing that is absolutely certain is that times are changing, and at an extremely rapid pace. This fact alarms many people who do not embrace change. American humorist Mark Twain once said, "The only person who likes change is a wet baby." People resist change and avoid situations where change is imminent. They do not desire to be participants in any change processes. Since we currently live in such volatilely changing times, the church needs to understand its purpose and overcome voices adverse to change.

President Ulysses S. Grant was introduced to the European game of golf by a gregarious Scotsman. The nervous instructor explained to the president of the United States the rules of the new game. Following the tutorial was a brief demonstration. He secured a golf ball from his bag and set it upon a tee. He then took a golf club and displayed a proper swing. As he completed the motion, his club hit into the ground, dirt spattered from the impact, but the ball was unmoved from the tee. The Scotsman repeated the attempt six consecutive times with the same embarrassing result on each try. Afterward President Grant musingly commented, "There seems to be a fair amount of exercise in the game, but I fail to see the purpose for the ball."

In vastly changing times such as these, many people fail to see the purpose of the church. What is the impetus for a church to gather? What promotes a cooperation of service for the community of faith? The answer is the commonality of our faith in the only unchanging reality: Jesus Christ. People from different nationalities, backgrounds, and experiences will all come together based upon the centrality of their trust in Jesus Christ, who "is the same yesterday, today, and forever" (Heb. 13:8).

The modern church must clearly understand its environment to be effective. "From the Issacharites, who understood the times and knew what Israel should do . . ." (1 Chron. 12:32). To provide context for this passage, Saul, the king of Israel, recently died because he was unfaithful to the Lord. The king had consulted a fortune-teller for counsel rather than going to God. This obvious act of unfaithfulness led to his premature death.

After his death, David became king, providing a new sense of direction and purpose for the kingdom. The Scripture proceeds with a synopsis of David's army giving details of each group's strengths. In the midst of this laborious list of tribes that were preparing for battle, we are introduced to a little-known sect named the Issacharites. This passage in the Bible provides a rare evaluation of the group's two greatest attributes. They were *socially perceptive* and they *understood their times.*

Staying current and understanding one's times can be an extremely difficult task. Listed below are five modern-day perceptions of the church. These assumptions are not very flattering, but to be effective the current church must comprehend them.

1. *Churches are not connecting people to God.* One-third of all Americans say church is not relevant to them.[16] One-third of all young people currently attending church declare that when they live apart from their parents, they will not continue going to church, because the church doesn't seem relevant to them. This damaging perception is potentially deadly to the church if not dealt with and corrected in the near future.[17]

2. *Churches are not cognizant of their neighbors.* A disturbing statistic is that 24 percent (less than one-in-four people) outside of the church know a Christian personally. Atheists and agnostics obviously do not frequently

befriend believers. But if you take them out of the statistical mix, among the rest of those surveyed, 60 percent *still* do not know a Christian personally. Fifty-three percent of Americans say they know a homosexual. Therefore, more unchurched people in America know a homosexual personally than know an evangelical Christian by name.[18] The modern church has been in seclusion for decades. Churches are just not cognizant of their neighbors.

3. *Churches are seldom cross-cultural in their approach.* In the latest statistical data for the city of Duluth, 30 percent of our residents were born outside of the United States.[19] Our schools are cross-cultural. Our restaurants are cross-cultural. Our shops and retail outlets are cross-cultural. But sadly, for the most part, our churches have remained monocultural.

4. *Churches are closing at an alarming rate.* I learned this alarming statistic concerning my own denomination's demise in the metro Atlanta area. There were 166 Southern Baptist churches inside the perimeter of Atlanta in 1966. I remember when I was a seminary student in the early 1980s, the one place every seminary student desired to establish a ministry was in Atlanta. The city was known for large churches that were burgeoning in attendance and spawning new church plants at a phenomenal pace. Of those 166 Southern Baptist churches that existed in 1966, only 39 of them are still in existence today. Churches are closing at an alarming rate. It is a sad state of affairs to observe churches that have lost their influence and impact upon their local community. A

drive through the metro area will discover churches that have closed their doors and sold their buildings. These church casualties no longer have any influence on the local community.[20]

5. *Churches are not really concerned about human suffering, poverty, the widows and orphans, or the exploited.* Churches have a tendency to bury our heads in the sand. Fact: *Atlanta Daily World* named Atlanta the capital of sexual exploitation in America. Fact: Atlanta is known as the number-one hub of human trafficking and child sexual exploitation in the United States. Fact: Men travel from across the world to come to Atlanta in order to exploit our young people.[21]

In the Old Testament it was the Issacharites who stuck their head out the window, rather than in the sand, and understood their times. If that had been their only accomplishment, many would not be very impressed, but the remainder of the passage claims that the Issacharites knew what to do.

Leadership guru John Maxwell says the greatest separator in our world is action. There are those who do, and there are those who do not. So be a doer! Psychologists claim there are three situations where people tend to act the least like themselves: When one walks into the lobby of an expensive hotel, one walks differently; when one shops in a new car showroom, one talks differently; when one sits down in the pew of a church, one acts differently.

Five Motives

Churches are filled with *pretenders* when they need to be filled with *contenders*. Jesus confronted this early in His ministry. "Not everyone who says to Me, 'Lord, Lord!' will enter the kingdom of heaven, but only the one who does the will of My Father in heaven" (Matt. 7:21). The Bible instructs believers to be doers and not just hearers. At First Baptist Church, we have established five motives around which we have centered our entire worship experience. This is why we do what we do (see Appendix B).

A Worshiping Community

First, we are a worshiping community, because God created us and desires for us to be in relationship with Him and with others. "The people I formed for Myself will declare My praise" (Isa. 43:21). Seventy-five percent of all adults in America (and 92 percent of people inside the church) say worship is of utmost importance in their life. Even among people who do not go to church, worship is a value.

Leonard Sweet, professor of evangelism at Drew Theological School, once said, "Worship should be EPIC. *E:* it should be experiential. *P:* it should be participatory. *I:* it should be image-rich. *C:* it should be connective."[22] Churches should connect people with one another, and they should connect people with God.

At First Baptist Church, we have committed to be a worshiping community. We have evaluated the facilities of all of our worship spaces and are renovating all of the worship spaces in our church, not just our sanctuary but our youth worship space and our children's worship space, indicating to everyone that worship is important to us, because we desire to connect with God.

A Missional Community

Second, we are a missional community, because our world needs a demonstration of God's forgiving and healing love in words and in actions. "By this all people will know that you are My disciples, if you have love for one another" (John 13:35). It pains me to think only one-in-five people know a believer in Jesus Christ. In response to this sad reality, FBC Duluth has taken the posture of being highly visible community leaders. We desire to volunteer in public schools, partner with the city government on projects, and be a high-profile promoter of anything beneficial to our locale.

We have adopted BB Harris Elementary School and pledged our volunteer base to aid in any way toward their success. BB Harris is a Title I school where 40 percent of the school's student body is under the U.S. definition of low income. Sixty-nine percent of BB Harris students are on free or government-subsidized reduced lunch. First Baptist Church has provided school supplies and backpacks for disadvantaged children and we service their families though our food pantry ministry. Each Thanksgiving, families within our church—including children of all ages—come to the church Monday through Wednesday for the purpose of preparing a traditional turkey dinner for over a hundred local families! These meals are personally delivered—fully cooked and ready to eat—on Thanksgiving morning to local, preselected homes. I personally believe it would be a sin to know that four-in-five people in my community do not know a Christian and yet do nothing to remedy the situation.

An Inclusive Community

Third, we are an inclusive community, because following Jesus demands we overcome barriers of gender, language, ethnicity, class, age, and culture. "If I am lifted up from the earth I will draw all people to Myself" (John 12:32).

Since 30 percent of Duluthians were born outside the United States, we have developed a multi-language ministry known as the One Voice Interpretation Center. This ministry was initiated years ago with the establishment of ESL (English as a Second Language) classes. These classes are often the first experience an immigrant has with an American church or even their first experience with Christians. Classes are taught weekly, free of charge, by a passionate group of trained volunteers who portray the love of Christ to these new residents.

Classes have now expanded beyond teaching English to newcomers. We are now offering "Spanish on Mission." Hispanics comprise the largest non-English local people group. Therefore, there is an acute interest in learning how to converse and ultimately witness with my Spanish neighbors. Also, because of our strong Hispanic ties, First Baptist Church is partnering in church planting efforts in Mexico, sending volunteer teams every year to support the work. Offering regular Spanish classes has proven invaluable in preparing for these cross-cultural outreach efforts.

This year has seen the creation of our third language offering at FBCD: Korean. Many Korean churches offer Saturday Korean classes for next-generation members of their extended family. These classes promote preservation of heritage and culture among this proud and family-centric people group. Our church staff began to evaluate how we could provide a similar experience for the growing number of Korean families that were beginning to attend FBCD. After some forethought and prayer, God provided our fellowship with a retired Korean school principle, experienced in establishing Korean language schools across the United States. However, this was to be her first such offering in an English-dominant church. These classes will provide the language preservation sought by Korean families as well as a cross-cultural ministry element for Americans and other international students. One of my greatest joys has been to observe Lucy, a Korean native first introduced to the church through the ESL class. She is now a regular student of the Spanish on Mission class and works the registration desk for the Saturday Korean classes.

Another element of the One Voice Interpretation Center ministry is the provision of simultaneous translation offered during the Sunday morning worship service. It has been our long-term goal to eventually offer these services in Duluth's three primary non-English-speaking languages (Korean, Spanish, and Chinese). To date, we have trained interpreters each Sunday for Spanish and Korean, and we are working toward a partnership with a Chinese missionary organization to provide needed personnel for our third language. We are committing ourselves to the miracle of Pentecost where people heard the Word of God in their own native tongue.

The Day of Pentecost is often misinterpreted. Many think the miracle was that people spoke in unknown languages, but Acts 2:8 clearly states that people *heard* in their own native tongue. "How is it that each of us can hear in our own native language?" This phenomenon now happens every week at First Baptist

Church Duluth, thanks to God's provision of a few exceptionally gifted linguists.

A Generous Community

Fourth, we are a generous community because of our gratitude for the generosity of God. "But just as you excel in everything . . . see that you also excel in this grace [of giving]" (2 Cor. 8:7). Giving is a part of the very character of God. Therefore, anyone desiring to follow God will also desire to give unconditionally, just as He has to the world. At First Baptist Church, we have come to realize the far-reaching global impact of our relatively small band of believers. Learning the lesson of giving has unleashed the powerful potential for the church.

Our church is not a megachurch, nor do we have the resources of a megachurch. So we are partnering with the North American Mission Board of the Southern Baptist Convention to sponsor church-planting efforts in our sister city of Duluth, Minnesota, as well as supporting local church planters in the suburban Atlanta area. Our great desire is to replicate what God has accomplished in our suburban context in other strategic areas, hoping to ignite a multiplying movement of multicultural churches.

First Baptist Church is providing financial and people resources to establish church-planting efforts in Mexico, India, Nigeria, and the United States. A future partnership establishing house churches in China is being prayerfully investigated at this time. These are financially challenging days for many church ministries. The initial reaction to financial shortfall is often to preserve ministries already established and halt any new endeavors. This practice more resembles hoarding than the biblical example of giving.

A Just Community

Finally, we are a just community because following Jesus involves confronting the world's evils and restoring biblical truth or justice. "What it is the LORD requires of you: to act justly, to love faithfulness, and to walk humbly with your God" (Micah 6:8). First Baptist Church Duluth is addressing the problem of human trafficking in our area by partnering with local organizations like Street Grace and the END IT Movement. The church also supports Wellspring Living, a local ministry providing living support for women that have broken free from abusive situations.

My daughter Rachel is a CPA at an Atlanta firm. During a March visit at our home Rachel recounted her day in the office. "I realize I'm not the most sports-minded individual, but in the office this week one of the ladies came up to me and asked, 'What's this March Madness thing all about?'" For those suffering from the same basketball oblivion, March Madness is the college basketball championship tournament, always played in the month of March.

People are fanatical about March Madness. Reserved captains of industry will paint team colors on their face, others will travel hundreds of miles to attend tournament games. I have observed people shouting at their television set as if they were present at the game. My prayer for some time has been that the church would exhibit far greater enthusiasm for the path God has laid out for us than for March Madness. At FBC Duluth, we have fostered the notion that these changing times we live in are not an excuse to back away from ministry, but to boldly and enthusiastically step to the front and lead. Stick your head out the window and you might see a cross-cultural ministry movement parading down your street.

▼ ▼ ▼

The Biblical Practices
of Multicultural Ministry

CHAPTER SIX

▼ ▼ ▼

Piñatas, Dumplings, Cricket, and Coffee

The Celebrations
of Multicultural Ministry

Rejoice with those who rejoice; weep with those who weep. Be in agreement with one another. Do not be proud; instead, associate with the humble. Do not be wise in your own estimation. (Romans 12:15–16)

What is the first step for a monocultural church in creating a multiethnic community? Unfortunately, many well-meaning ministries begin a ministry *to* the various people groups of their locale rather than a ministry *with* the diverse population of their community. This can be summarized as the difference in being *for you* and *with you*. The commitment to be with someone is a far deeper commitment, but worth it. There are three distinct advantages of being *with*.

The Advantages of Being *With*

Proximity

Several years ago I had the opportunity to purchase season tickets for our local professional football team, the Atlanta Falcons. A friend of my son-in-law purchased a new automobile—a KIA. The local dealership was having a promotion of free season tickets with a new car purchase. The new car owner, not a football fan, was seeking a buyer for his newfound windfall. The tickets were first offered to Mike, my son-in-law, at a ridiculously inexpensive price. When I learned that Mike had declined the offer, I pleaded with him to call back and to purchase the tickets on my behalf. When I studied the team's home schedule of eight games, I calculated I could attend at least four of them, and finding interested buyers for the other four games at the current cost per ticket seemed very likely.

I have been a professional football fan since childhood, and through the years, I have had the opportunity to attend some games. But now, I was a season ticket holder! I was filled with anticipation to attend my first Falcons game, a Thursday night matchup against legendary quarterback Peyton Manning and the Denver Broncos. I was enthused to the point of childhood giddiness as my wife, Glenda, and I arrived an hour before game time. We made the long trek from the parking lot to the Georgia Dome. Once inside, we began the search for our seats: Section 338, Row 26, Seats 3 and 4. It is a good thing that we allotted extra time in our schedule. Our journey took us to the upper deck to find our section entrance, and then we began the steep climb to Row 26, the last row inside the stadium. Our seats were in the corner of the end zone, in the upper deck, all the way against the wall of the mammoth seventy-one-thousand-capacity Georgia Dome. Suddenly I realized why a car dealership was giving these tickets away as an incentive!

I settled into my "season ticket" seats to enjoy the game. From the very opening kickoff, a gentleman adjacent to us began a tirade. He was yelling at the referees and criticizing the coaches with occasional vulgar, obscene language. Alas, the first timeout caused a break in the game and every attendee retook their seats for a momentary respite before action resumed. The angry gentleman looked over at my wife and I and asked, "So, did you buy a KIA?"

This man was a Falcon fanatic. He was *for* the team and he went *to* the game. Down on the playing surface there were actual Falcon players and coaches. These personnel are *with* the Falcons. Being with someone requires proximity.

Promise

I once heard a story about a family with three young children that begged their parents for a gerbil. The mother was slow to approve the household pet for fear the children would not take on the responsibility of caring for the new family member. She finally acquiesced to the idea, the children picked out their new pet, and they named him Danny. Soon after Danny's arrival, as the mother had forewarned, the total burden of the gerbil's care was placed upon her. After a particularly trying day, the mother exploded with disappointment in her children's lack of care. "No one cleans up after him; he eats everything in the house; Danny is going to have to go!" declared the mom. The children were devastated!

They began to plead in negotiations with their mother. "What if he eats less? What if we promise to help more?" But the mother was persistent and firm in her resolve: "Danny has got to go!" The children stopped crying and seemed somewhat relieved. The eldest explained, "Ohhhhh, we thought you said 'Daddy.' It's okay if Danny has to leave!"

The marriage vows say, "For better or worse." Being with someone is a commitment of the heart, no matter the circumstances. On my Facebook profile I have hundreds of friends. It is a very limited commitment to be a Facebook friend with someone. But the profile also indicates that I'm married. There is a big difference between the degree of promise of a Facebook friend and that of a committed spouse. Glenda and I have been *with* each other for over thirty-five years. We've been together through trials and triumphs, because being *with* involves a greater promise.

Power

I recall a children's message illustration when I was young that had a lasting impact on me. The pastor handed each of us two tongue depressors. He asked each of us to take the first one and test our strength to see if we could snap it in two. The boys of the groups were quick to flex our muscles and express how easy the assigned task was to complete. However, girls and boys alike were capable of accomplishing the simple request. The parabolic teaching proceeded when the pastor requested to collect all the remaining tongue depressors, one from each child present. Once gathered, a rubber band was placed around the stack of approximately twenty sticks. The pastor then challenged, "Who is able to break the accumulation of depressors?" Each individual took a turn to try this feat of strength, but none were able to accomplish the task. The life lesson to be learned is there is strength in numbers and there is power in being *with* others.

I believe the power of "with" is the lesson of Romans 12. This is the philosophy that informs First Baptist Church Duluth as we develop cross-cultural relationships and introduce ourselves to our multiethnic community. Author and commentator Dr. John Phillips referred to the process of celebrating with people as developing "redemptive friendships."[23] It pains me to think of the number of believers that do not associate with one single non-Christian friend. People are fearful of such liaisons. Many will ask, "What will we have to talk about? What if I say the wrong thing?" Adding the increased complexity of crossing a cultural barrier makes these friendships intricately complicated.

How does one initiate a redemptive friendship? Perhaps it's like the strategy for a game of dominos. The object of dominos is to match the tile pieces of your opponent until one player runs out of dominos and wins the game. The apostle Paul would have been a domino champion, because the game describes the heart of his entire ministry.

> Although I am a free man and not anyone's slave, I have made myself a slave to everyone, in order to win more people. To the Jews I became like a Jew, to win Jews; to those under the law, like one under the law—though I myself am not under the law—to win those under the law. To those who are without that law, like one without the law—not being without God's law but within Christ's law—to win those without the law. (1 Cor. 9:19–21)

Paul found ways to strategically connect to every segment of society in order to share the gospel with all people.

Different cultures celebrate in different ways, but everyone loves a party! Celebrating across cultural lines tears down barriers and opens lines of communication. Jesus was a frequent guest at wedding parties, banquets, and an assortment of other celebratory occasions. Perhaps we should learn from the biblical examples of the apostle Paul and Jesus Himself, and seek ways to celebrate with the various people groups in our local community.

In August 2012, the summer Olympics were in full swing in London. I recall watching the majestic opening ceremonies as the athletes marched into the stadium bearing the flag of their country. This pageantry is beautiful and emotionally moving. As I observed, I pondered, *How many countries are currently represented in the membership of First Baptist Church Duluth? And what if we had a parade of flags to show our solidarity around the cause of Jesus Christ?* After a couple of weeks of internal research, we surmised that there were twenty countries represented in our church body. On the Sunday of the closing ceremonies of the Olympic Games, we had our own parade of flags at First Baptist Church as we sang the Newsboys song "He Reigns," about God's people from every tribe, tongue, and nation worshipping Him.

As each flag appeared in the procession, it was carried by a proud native of its homeland. By the conclusion, when all twenty flags were at the front of the sanctuary, people were shouting and cheering in praise to the Almighty! Reaction after the service was overwhelmingly positive. Some informed me they had no idea the international complexion of our congregation. Others said they sensed the very presence of heaven as every nation was surrendering to the Lord Jesus Christ. Many felt we had experienced the type of worship described in Revelation 7.

Since that transitional day in the life of our church, the flags have become a permanent fixture in our sanctuary. Placed along the perimeter of our balcony, the number has now grown to thirty-five.[24] The weekly worship guide publication has an explanation for all newcomers: "The 40 flags on display in the Worship Center represent the 'birth nations' of our church and Sunday school members. If your flag does not appear, please notify the church office to remedy our error." Over these past four years I have observed first-time guests walk the circumference of our sanctuary in search of their native flag. "Is there someone in this fellowship that is from my same area of the world?" Guests have indicated that their flag is omitted and I have responded, "Come be a part of us as the first person from _____." When an international comes for membership at the end of a service, we indicate the presence of their flag or we inform the congregation a new flag is to be presented; God is opening another opportunity for ministry.

As the congregation has become increasingly diverse, we have sought ways to celebrate our cultural diversity and learn from each other. Three annual celebrations now dot our church calendar as community events that aid the church to "rejoice with those who rejoice."

Annual Church Celebrations

Indian Independence Day

The first attempt at cross-cultural celebration for FBC Duluth was Indian Independence Day, celebrated on August 15, 2013, and annually since. There is a growing population of Indian natives in our locale. So much so that a Hindu temple has been erected about one hundred yards from our church facility. Many of these families have sought the services of our weekday preschool. Indian nationals are currently the third largest people group in our weekday ministry. The Indian families within our church fellowship are deeply committed to the cause of Christ and desire to make an impact upon the South Asian portion of our community.

An assembly of the four active Indian families of our fellowship was arranged in early 2013 for the purpose of planning a community-wide celebration for Indian Independence Day. Much like the American Fourth of July, India celebrates their independence from years of being a British territory. The first year of our celebration we had a street festival on the front parking lot of the church. Indian food was served alongside inflatable games for the children and a henna art booth for people to sample the Indian culture. In subsequent years, an Indian fashion show has been held, a Christian sitar artist has played a concert, and an Indian dance team has been formed—comprised of all non-Indians with the exception of the founder of the group.

This past year's celebration may have solicited our largest gathering of Indian nationals. On a Saturday afternoon we served high tea, a purely British tradition mostly foreign to the typical American. High tea is to be served in the late afternoon, almost like the appetizer for a late dinner. It is a respected time of interaction, fellowship, and a reminder of all that is civil in the world. Our gracious Indian families hosted the tea with delightful Indian foods and, thankfully, they included warnings about extremely spicy cuisines! The tea was an informal affair at our church picnic pavilion and was attended by individuals from a great variety of ages and cultures. At the conclusion of high tea, there was a cricket demonstration on our church athletic fields. Children and adults were invited to participate to learn the rules of a game that seems similar to American baseball, but is completely different. A number of Hindu men attended at our invitation to teach their national pastime to the American crowd. It was delightful to observe the bonds formed by a simple game that allowed us to rejoice with those that rejoice.

Three Kings Day (Tres Reyes Magos)

Christmas of 2014 brought about our second cross-cultural celebration. Three Kings Day is a predominantly Latin American holiday celebrated on January 6. This Spanish tradition is based upon the biblical account of the magi found in Matthew chapter 2, where kings brought gifts to baby Jesus of gold, frankincense, and myrrh. Because of the three gifts, many have speculated that they were kings. Before going to bed on the eve of January 6, children polish their shoes and leave them ready for the kings to place presents in them. The next morning children awake to gifts in their shoes. If they have misbehaved during the year they receive coal—usually a lump of hard sugar candy dyed black called carbón dulce. In Hispanic cultures, children once received gifts on this day instead of Christmas. Now, in most countries, children receive gifts on both days.

One of the treats of Three Kings Day is the *Rosca de Reyes*—a ring shaped Epiphany cake—that is eaten as all the Christmas decorations are being put away. Placed inside the cake is a plastic figurine of the baby Jesus. The one who locates the king doll in their serving of cake is supposed to host the rest of the party guests at his or her home for dinner within the next week. The celebrations of Three Kings Day can be traced back to Spain as early as AD 1164.

The Spanish-speaking members of First Baptist Church Duluth have hosted this event annually. This past year's celebration included a mariachi band and an authentic Mexican taco truck dinner. Christmas carols were performed in Spanish by a group of English-speaking members participating in Spanish classes at the church. Children were asked to take their shoes off and line them against the wall in anticipation of the kings' appearance. The gospel story of Christmas is shared in English and interpreted in Español for all to hear. The *Rosca de Reyes* is served to each table with a king doll discovered for each group. After recognizing the winners of the coveted doll at each table, we inform them of the tradition to invite everyone to your house for dinner within the next week. The winners are then informed that to rescue them from embarrassment, Chick-fil-A has provided a coupon for every person present.

At the conclusion of the night, three young men dressed as the kings appear in the crowd bringing gift bags to place in the awaiting assemblage of shoes. The culmination of the evening is to bust a piñata filled with candy to the delight of every child present. This cross-cultural event mixes the traditions of a variety of countries and has introduced a number of people to the eclectic nature of our church family. It is a truly fun night to rejoice with those who rejoice.

Korean/Chinese New Year

Most Asian cultures celebrate New Year on the lunar calendar instead of the solar calendar. Therefore, in China, Mongolia, Tibet, Vietnam, Japan, and Korea, the New Year begins in early February rather than on January 1. Each country has celebration traditions unique to their culture. Korea is a very family-oriented society. Millions of citizens travel to their native city to spend time with family for the holiday. A large family feast is prepared, equivalent to American Thanksgiving traditions. Children and adults alike adorn themselves with colorful Korean clothing to add to the festive atmosphere.

In China, preparations for New Year include a thorough cleaning of the house to rid the home of bad luck or ill fortune. Windows and doors are decorated with bright red paper cutouts to usher in good luck to the family. Fireworks—a Chinese invention—are often the culmination of the evening's festivities.

Although each country's traditions are distinct, there are two common themes I found across cultural lines. First, each has an element of honoring the elderly. There is an opportunity to pay tribute to the oldest generation of the family. The second cross culturally consistent theme is the arrival of new life. The New Year is a celebration of the coming of spring and the earth returning to life. Both of these concepts are deeply rooted in Scripture.

Clearly the Bible teaches us to honor our elders. "Honor your father and mother which is the first commandment with a promise, so that it may go well with you and that you may live a long life in the land" (Eph. 6:2–3). The Bible also celebrates the new life that is available to all of us through Jesus Christ. "Therefore, if anyone is in Christ, he is a new creation; old things have passed away, and look, new things have come" (2 Cor. 5:17).

Our first effort to celebrate Korean/Chinese New Year at FBC Duluth was 2016. Recognizing the elements of traditional celebrations as well as the complexity of a holiday representative of so many cultural groups, we initiated our plans. We have three Korean natives on church staff that aided immensely in establishing a meaningful event. The church's celebration was centered around the two themes previously described: honoring our elders and celebrating new life.

Cindy Rhe, a Korean native, established a traditional Korean Fan Dance Team. Complete with authentic costumes on loan from the Korean Consulate's office, this team practiced hours and hours to present a beautiful portrayal of new life. The dance was choreographed to a very popular Christian song from Korea and concluded with the fans forming the shape of a cross, portraying the source of genuine new life. All congregation members present over the age of eighty were asked to come to the front of the auditorium and sit in seats of honor as the "special guests" for the dance troupe.

During the staff meetings in preparation for this event, Tom Rhe, the church's ministry intern, mentioned a possibility of the Korean Consulate recognizing and honoring veterans of the Korean War. I thought this to be a grand idea and expected that the Consulate would possibly produce a "Certificate of Appreciation" that we could pass on to these war veterans. Research began internally and somewhat secretly as to the names of church members who served the military during the early 1950s in support of the war effort. To our surprise, we located nine veterans of the conflict that took place over sixty years prior! The Consulate returned our request by providing an "Ambassador Medal of Peace" for each war hero.

This beautiful medallion is presented in gratitude for the service of securing the freedom of South Korea. The Consulate's office informed me that this presentation would be the first of their knowledge to ever take place in an American church service. Each medal was accompanied with a personalized proclamation that read as follows:

> It is a great honor and pleasure to express the everlasting gratitude of the Republic of Korea and our people for the service you and your countrymen have performed in restoring and preserving our freedom and democracy.
>
> We cherish in our hearts the memory of your boundless sacrifices in helping us establish our Free Nation.
>
> In grateful recognition of your dedicated contributions, it is our privilege to proclaim you an "AMBASSADOR FOR PEACE" with every good wish of people of the Republic of Korea. Let each of us reaffirm our mutual respect and friendship that they may endure for generations to come.

The proclamation is signed by the Minister of Patriots and Veterans Affairs for the Republic of Korea and the Chairman of the Korean Veterans Association. In anticipation of this presentation, the church informed families of the nine veterans that something historic in nature would be happening on the assigned Sunday.

The Korean Consulate offered to send a designee to award the medals at our Korean/Chinese New Year celebratory service. However, Tom Rhe declined their offer in favor of a more meaningful and powerfully integrating concept. On the morning of the awards, the medallions would be presented by the Korean families of the congregation with the next generation—children of the Korean members—physically placing the medals around the necks of each war hero. This was a phenomenal picture of respect, honor, and tribute. One veteran told me after the service that he had never been honored in such a beautiful manner. Another talked with pride about the Korean children continuously saying "thank you" to him and his fellow servicemen.

This wedding of cultures will become our third annual celebratory event at First Baptist Church Duluth. After the service, all were invited to a catered Chinese lunch in our dining facility. Chinese members had informed us that the food of celebration in China is the Chinese dumpling, so a variety of dumplings was on the menu to sample and enjoy. A Korean folk singer performed dinner music for the gathering.

These three events have provided the impetus for cross-cultural interactions and have established connections within our community. The church sought ways to continue these healthy cross-cultural conversations beyond the limitations of awaiting the next major scheduled event.

International Grounds Café

Coffee shops tend to be the point of connection in many American communities. Business meetings take place over a cup of coffee. Reunions of friends happen many times at a coffeehouse. Good news is celebrated with a cup of coffee and bad news is tolerated with a cup of coffee. Once inside a coffeehouse, the careful observer will note the depth of interaction that is taking place. Friendships are being formed. Emotional healing is taking place. And healthy interaction is happening that fosters a development of good will.

In an attempt to sustain the efforts brought about by the dynamic cultural events at FBC Duluth, we built a café in the main guest entrance to our facility. The name of the facility celebrates our church's diversity and cements our heart for the nations. The coffee shop is called International Grounds Café. This has quickly become a place to meet people before and after church service or to establish a future meeting time and place.

All of the coffees and teas served in the café are international products. The coffee is supplied by a ministry that funds church-planting efforts in the Third World and provides above-average wages for coffee farmers. Local proceeds go to our church's mission fund, supporting our church planters and partnership projects. With every coffee purchase, the kingdom of God is being blessed.

Prior to opening the café, our church had a meet-and-greet time with my wife and me after the church service for all guests present that day. This informal gathering took place in a room behind the sanctuary where we would present each newcomer with a gift bag and a hospitable *thank you for being with us today.* This after-church ritual has been relocated to the new International Grounds Café, and has been aptly named the After Church Party. Before, my wife and I would struggle to garner the attention of a limited number of guests that would make the effort to come to a meet-and-greet. Now, dozens of members stay and interact with newcomers in an atmosphere that is inviting and exhilarating. I have observed people meeting for the first time, sitting for extended periods in deep conversation. Since the relocation of the after-church event, the number of recognized guests has quadrupled. What is the difference? The personal interaction that breaks down every preventive barrier is the key.

These events have galvanized the entire congregation into a genuine cross-cultural team that is ready and willing to invite people of all ethnicities to "my church." Our leadership team is always looking for additional meaningful opportunities to cross barriers and provide an avenue for cross-cultural interaction. As I write this, my mind is racing as to what could potentially be the next event that opens a new door of opportunity within our community.

CHAPTER SEVEN

▼ ▼ ▼

There's a Monkey in the Pulpit!

The Conflicts of Multicultural Ministry

So we must not get tired of doing good, for we will reap
at the proper time if we don't give up. (Galatians 6:9)

The Bible clearly teaches that conflict in this world is inevitable.
Jesus said, "In the world you will have tribulation; but be of
good cheer, I have overcome the world" (John 16:33 NKJV). Even
though conflict is inevitable, people go to great lengths to avoid
it. The path of multicultural ministry is particularly difficult
for those averse to conflict. Rest assured, people will staunchly
oppose the path of multiculturalism!

In the summer of 2014, Laura Meckler, a writer with the *Wall
Street Journal,* contacted me about an article she was developing about the changing face of church in America. In our initial
phone interview, she was elated to learn of the multicultural

approach of our church and asked if she could come for an onsite visit with a photographer to document for her upcoming story. Laura also asked for the contact information of additional church leaders to interview in preparation for the publication. We greatly anticipated our esteemed media visitors. But they never came. Laura notified me that our church was going to be included in the article, but was not going to be the feature. Her reasoning was that after interviewing several church leaders within our fellowship, she surmised that our church was in the "Kumbaya stage" of multicultural ministry. Many of us remember sitting next to a bonfire at church camp and singing "kum-ba-ya." Laura was saying that our church was in the midst of the almost sublime, naïve state that is often associated with this song. She explained that our church had not yet wrestled with the real struggles that multicultural ministry brings. Her interviews had revealed an excited naiveté from leaders that the church is for all people and will, therefore, gladly welcome all people. Little did I realize at the time how prophetic her words and warning were.[25] Our multicultural path had not been significantly opposed or challenged up to that time.

Facing Conflict

Within a year of the *Wall Street Journal* article, First Baptist Church Duluth began to see extraordinary new member growth among internationals. This greatly stretched the comfort level of many existing members and caused some consternation. In the spring of 2015, I received the following unsigned letter in my church mailbox. Typically, I do not keep such blatantly negative correspondence. However, this letter has been a reminder and a rallying cry for what is really important in our church ministry.

Pastor, my family and I have listened to you talk about multicultural and multiethnic since you came here. Enough! Enough talking about it. Stop forcing it down people's throats. They are gagging on it. When you say we are going to be a multicultural church, you are putting a label on every person in the building. If you have to "incorporate" something into a service to make it a multicultural service, then you are forcing something that just isn't there. Now, I am not saying that heaven won't be like that . . . that it won't have different languages and that isn't important . . . I am not saying those things. What I am saying is ENOUGH! We are tired of hearing about it and how amazingly wonderful the multicultural people in our church are. They aren't any different than the rest of us who have been serving in this place for years.

I have been praying all week and looking forward to Easter, although I heard that the service for Sunday Night Live (a Palm Sunday special service) is going to involve dancing and people speaking in their "heart language." I know you think that's wonderful, but parading them around to show off our multi-ethnicity just looks like a circus performance. *I'll let you decide which animal you are.*

Reading this letter was like taking a punch in the gut. I expected opposition concerning our methodologies, but I was deeply wounded that someone would question my motives.

Rather than disregarding the letter as the tirade of an extremely disgruntled and angry member, I sought the counsel of several close minister colleagues as well as a few key church leaders. Many people do not open or read unsigned mail because of the lack of ability to meaningfully deal with content without knowing the agendas of the author. Nonetheless, I wanted to know if there was a genuine issue with how the congregation perceived this new direction set before them.

Don't Unhinge the Bow

During this time of introspection, I rediscovered a favorite Bible verse: "So we must not get tired of doing good, for we will reap at the proper time if we don't give up" (Gal. 6:9). The phrase "don't give up" in the Holman Christian Standard Bible translation is "faint not" in the King James Version. This is a rich picture-word in the New Testament Greek language. It is a word that literally means to "unhinge the bow." A first-century archer did little shooting for sport or leisure. The reason for drawing back an arrow into the bow most likely would have been for food or survival. For the person who has never attempted archery, the process seems simple and not very physically demanding. Nothing could be further from the truth. It takes tremendous upper body strength to draw the arrow into a taut bow. To hold it in that position for any significant amount of time is physically demanding to the point of absolute exhaustion. A reader of the letter to the Galatians would probably recall a time on the hunt when, holding the bow in ready position waiting for the proper shot, the demand was overwhelming and he just had to unhinge the bow. As I read this verse with fresh eyes, I heard the encouragement of God's

Spirit: "Mark, you can't give up. You can't unhinge the bow. The cause is too great and the stakes are too high!"

Because of our involvement in mission causes in India, I read the testimony of famed missionary William Carey. This patriarch of the modern missionary movement arrived in India in 1793 passionate and ready to preach the gospel. But it took *seven* years before the first person became a Christian under his ministry. Carey documented his struggle with discouragement in his journal: "I feel as a farmer does about his crop. Sometimes I think the seed is springing and thus I hope . . . and my hopes are gone like a cloud. Yet I still hope in God and will go forth in His strength."[26] On December 28, 1800, William Carey baptized in the Ganges River his first convert, Krishna Pal. Thus began one of the greatest missionary movements in world history. One of the Indian families in our church shared with me their lineage as direct descendants of converts of the ministry of the persistent missionary Carey. William Carey's tenacity to not give up in the face of overwhelming discouragement continues to impact the world to this day.

Why Do People Give Up?

There are two primary reasons people tend to give up on a project. They are enumerated in the book of Hebrews.

> Therefore, since we also have such a large crowd of witnesses surrounding us, let us lay aside every weight and the sin that so easily ensnares us. Let us run with endurance the race that lies before us, keeping our eyes on Jesus, the source and perfecter of our faith, who for the joy that lay before Him endured a cross and despised the shame

and has sat down at the right hand of God's throne. For consider Him who endured such hostility from sinners against Himself, so that you won't *grow weary and lose heart*. (Heb. 12:1–3, emphasis mine)

Some people quit because they have grown weary. One cannot confuse laziness with weariness. People grow weary when their physical, emotional, and mental energy spent exceeds their ability to replenish in adequate supply. This does not mean somebody is lazy; in fact, it often means the exact opposite.

One of the chief lessons I have learned in the pursuit of multicultural ministry has been the difficulty of the path. The work of multicultural ministry is similar to that of a trailblazer. We are called to cut a road where no road previously existed. This is taxing work that must be entered into with clarity of direction and expectations of opposition. This work is not for the faint of heart. Many will lay down the task out of mental, emotional, and even physical exhaustion.

A second reason people tend to quit is because they lose heart. All of us have observed those passionate individuals who begin a project with great zeal, but later question the value of their involvement in the cause. I once heard a pastor describe such people in the church as "Alka-Seltzer Christians." You drop them in water (baptism), watch them fizzle for a little while, and then they disappear.[27] I certainly did not desire my pastoral leadership to be equated with this poor example of lackadaisical conviction.

Negative comments had not deterred me from the path of multicultural ministry. Although, admittedly, my eyes were now open to the fact that opposition was real and present. Volitionally,

I was leading forward with renewed scriptural fortitude to "not grow weary" or "lose heart," nor ultimately, to "unhinge the bow." Journalist Laura Meckler's assessment of our church was haunting me. Perhaps we had been living in the Kumbaya phase of our journey and now things were about to become confrontational.

Upping the Ante

I was increasingly committed to cross-cultural ministry. So much so, in fact, that I had asked a church member, Verdi Avila, to privately tutor me in Spanish. The goal was to eventually be capable of delivering a Sunday morning sermon in Español with him interpreting for the congregation. Instead of shrinking away in the face of conflict, I upped the ante.

I kept our sessions secretive for months because I had no idea when I would potentially be capable of accomplishing this monumental task. At times I grew frustrated, as learning a new language at my age is an exceedingly difficult task. However, I tried to keep my eyes set on the goal of communicating the gospel across a language barrier.

During the course of these private language lessons, the church was developing an interpretation ministry to offer real-time translation services of the Sunday morning services in Spanish, Korean, and eventually Mandarin Chinese. The date had been set for the first Sunday of June to unveil the One Voice Interpretation Center as a new ministry offered at FBCD. I thought this would be a great Sunday for me to reveal my months of practice and to preach the message in Spanish that morning as a picture parable of what it is like to be in a worship experience conducted in your secondary language. Having a set date deadline caused me to work harder toward the completion of my first ever Spanish sermon.

As the day arrived, I was nervous about the presentation of the morning message. On Sunday mornings, the church ministry staff gathers upon arrival at the building to complete necessary assignments and to pray together for God's guidance and blessing upon the day. The primary announcement of the morning was that the following week would be our church's annual Vacation Bible School. For readers not familiar with evangelical church life, Vacation Bible School is typically a one-week summer children's program with Bible stories, crafts, and games, all centered on a creative and fun theme. Our church has been holding VBS the first week after public schools break for the summer for years. The sanctuary is thematically decorated for hundreds of community children to arrive on Monday morning and successive mornings through the coming week.

Travis Boyd, our worship pastor, entered the staff prayer meeting with an announcement. "Don't be alarmed, but there's a monkey in the pulpit this morning." The humorous communique was a notification that the sanctuary had been decorated in a jungle theme in preparation for the upcoming Vacation Bible School sessions that week. And indeed, there was an inflatable monkey adorning the pulpit area. As I heard the announcement, my mind immediately reverted back to the unsigned letter from a few months earlier . . . *"I'll let you decide which animal you are."*

My upcoming message was my first attempt at preaching in Spanish, there was an unknown critic in the congregation that likened my ministry to a circus parade, and there was an inflatable monkey on the platform. I could not imagine a more potentially devastating cocktail of circumstances. I hid away in the church prayer room in the remaining time before the service started. I was more unnerved about the delivery of this message than any other in my more than thirty-five years in pastoral ministry. My heart cried out to God that the message would be perceived correctly and that He would be glorified.

As I arose to preach that morning, I introduced my interpreter Verdi Avila. I preached the introduction of the sermon in English as Verdi translated phrase-by-phrase into Spanish. I always conclude a sermon's introduction with the reading of Scripture and a prayer. At the conclusion of the pastoral prayer I began to preach in Spanish and Verdi translated into English. This unannounced turn of events caused amazement from the congregation, who had no idea of the plan. The message explained the events of the Day of Pentecost in Acts 2, when people miraculously began to hear the gospel in their own native languages. Spanish speakers in the congregation nodded with agreement as they graciously accepted my feeble attempt to communicate in their mother tongue. English speakers smiled as they were experiencing what every non-English worship participant encounters every week at our church.

The service was a great success. As is the case most weeks, we had numerous first-time guests in worship—many of them internationals. One particular family who was there for the first time stands out. This family is a cross-cultural marriage—he is a Hispanic from the Dominican Republic and she an Eastern European from Moldova. I later learned that she is employed as a high school Spanish teacher in our county—so glad I didn't know that intimidating fact ahead of my public attempt at bilingual ministry! Both were very complimentary of the gallant effort I made that morning and stated their desire to learn more about a church that was making concerted plans to be multicultural. This couple, Fernando and Silvia Rosario, later became members of FBCD and their testimony is shared in chapter 10.

Pressing On in Opposition

Satan attempts to discourage anyone and anything that is going to ultimately bring glory to God. "Be serious! Be alert! Your adversary the Devil is prowling around like a roaring lion, looking for anyone he can devour" (1 Pet. 5:8). Had I listened to the voice of discouragement, I would have never ventured to try and preach a sermon in Spanish. However, I believe this was a pivotal point in establishing our church as a multilingual congregation. Language is no longer an insurmountable barrier for our church within the community.

Be Resilient

For readers contemplating a journey into multicultural ministry, let me offer three words of advice for how to deal with imminent opposition. First, *be resilient*! Do not allow the mire of negativity to change a beautiful and God-given direction for your ministry. One of the greatest biblical examples of resilience is Joshua. After the death of Moses, this man of God was called to lead a rebellious people into the Promised Land. He might have been intimidated by the task, but the Lord spoke to Joshua: "Haven't I commanded you: be strong and courageous? Do not be afraid or discouraged, for the LORD your God is with you wherever you go" (Josh. 1:9). The Lord always provides encouragement along the path of obedience.

In July 2015, our local newspaper, the *Gwinnett Daily Post,* did a feature article on the diversity in our church.[28] In an attempt to increase readership of this good word, I posted a link to the article on my Facebook page. Positive comments came rampant across social media. One of them had a lasting effect on me.

One of our senior adult ladies, Jerri Joiner, reposted the article on her Facebook page. I was so honored that someone of her generation openly embraced the changes in our church and displayed them proudly for her friends to see. One of her friends commented on her post, and their exchange remains a source of strength and comfort for me to this day.

B: Reading this made me teary. Praises for Pastor Hearn.

Jerri: I like him very much. Our community is changing drastically and he is leading us through the changes. Praise the Lord. Otherwise our church would probably go the way of many others.

B: Jesus embraces us all, as should the church.

Jerri: You are 100 percent right. Change is always difficult for we seniors and Pastor Mark understands that and is just what we need.

Negativity was not going to have the victory in my life or in our church. God was providing affirmation of His plans and purposes.

Be Consistent

Second, *be consistent*! I have been approached on numerous occasions over the past five years and asked if our church would house an upstart language congregation. Because of the exponential growth of internationals in our area, language churches are in storefronts, empty homes, and any other available space in the community. I pass a dozen language congregations on my commute from my home to the FBCD facilities. It is sometimes difficult to explain to a passionate church planter our church's philosophy of ministry is that we can overcome the language barriers and worship as one body in Christ. It would be disingenuous for our church to tell guests that we are a church for every nation, every tribe, and every language group if there were another church meeting in another area of our facility that might meet their needs.

I believe that every language church serves a God-given purpose. My training, with a degree in the field of evangelism and another in the area of church growth, has taught me the homogeneous unit principle. This church growth tool is the concept that people with deepening degrees of like-mindedness are naturally attracted to each other. Spanish speakers desire to be among other Spanish speakers. Bankers tend to talk finances with other bankers. Golfers compare golf tales with other golfers. Although the homogeneous unit principle is an impactful tool for evangelism, it was never intended to be a blanket excuse for segregated worship.

It has been vital that our church remain faithful to our calling and on point when it comes to our message for the community. I have told several language church planters in search of aid that

FBCD would be far more apt to partner in evangelistic efforts than to forsake our philosophical moorings and send out a diluted image of our core values.

Be Persistent

Finally, *be persistent.* Resiliency will prevent you from quitting. Consistency will keep you on course. But persistency will ultimately achieve the goal. "I am sure of this, that He who started a good work in you will carry it on to completion until the day of Christ Jesus" (Phil. 1:6). Many a well-meaning minister has lost their passion during the fray of controversy and given up for lack of persistence. When this occurs, it is not because God has forsaken the work, but because the worker has forsaken God. Persistency is the hunger to see God's plan grow to fruition.

In the fall of this same year, I received a note of encouragement from one of our senior adult members, Olive Siegle. Affectionately known around the church as Ms. Olive, this octogenarian from Great Britain is a prayer warrior with the gift of encouragement. Ms. Olive handed me a card and said, "God gave me a word for you this week, Pastor . . . persistence."

As I was praying for you and our church, I received a word from the Lord: "Be not discouraged. The Lord God is with you" (1 Chronicles 28:20 NIV). You are doing exactly what Jesus commanded in the Great Commission (Matthew 28:18). I joined this church because of the direction in which you are guiding us. I believe strongly in it. Sometimes when God directs our path the road is rocky and we have to overcome obstacles in our way. Your last trip to India was a strong sign that you are on the right track. Do not falter but be passionate about what He is leading us toward.

I am an old lady and not really smart in financial things—but God has always found a way for me and He will for our church as well. I do know my gift is encouragement and so I use it freely. Be encouraged and know that the Lord thy God is with you! He will never leave you or forsake you.

I received this word for you on Monday evening and now it is Wednesday. I need to put this in your hands soon. God bless you and your family!

—Olive Siegle

Ms. Olive's reminder is one I will cherish for years. God has not forgotten about me! Stay the course and keep serving faithfully. Be persistent because He can even bless when there is a "monkey in the pulpit."

CHAPTER EIGHT

▼ ▼ ▼

It's Too Hard

The Complexities
of Multicultural Ministry

*Can you search through God's complex things? Can
you uncover the limits of the Almighty? (Job 11:7 ISV)*

My wife and I enjoy the television series *Elementary*. A modern-day remake of the adventures of Sherlock Holmes, this
drama series provides intriguing mystery mixed with satirical
dialogue. One of my favorite episodes is "Solve for X."[29] The story
line is the murder of a mathematician who is poised to provide
the answer to a previously declared impossible equation: "P ver-
sus NP." The episode intrigued me to the point that I did some
Internet research to discover if the equation was fictitious or,
indeed, a mathematical dilemma. I found the equation to be one
of the unsolved enigmas of computer science.

Is This Possible?

Unsolved mathematical equations simply affirm the finite nature of humanity in comparison to the infinite abilities of a Creator God. "Look, I am Yahweh, the God of all flesh. Is anything too difficult for Me?" (Jer. 32:27). There have been numerous occasions where people have attempted to instruct me that transitioning to a multicultural church model is an impossible task. In some respects, these people are right. *It is absolutely impossible for human beings to make this shift.* Fortunately, the outcome is not dependent upon our collective strength. Remember the admonition of Jesus to His disciples: "With men this is impossible, but with God all things are possible" (Matt. 19:26).

Releasing Issues

There are three complicated issues that I wish to share with anyone embarking upon this incredible journey. The first are *releasing issues.* Many immigrants are looking for people of similar culture to connect with in their new surroundings. Therefore, language churches in our area are plentiful. However, many of these churches are not growing. The reason is that maintenance of culture has taken precedence over expansion of the gospel and the creation of a genuine community of faith. This maintenance of culture prevents many language church pastors from understanding our concept of ministry and causes some to even question our motives in pursuing diversity.

At First Baptist Church Duluth, we have attempted to provide a path for internationals to embrace their culture while engaging in an eclectic style of worship and ministry that celebrates all nations gathering to praise Christ. An example of this is the formation of the Duluth Culture Center, a weekday program for Korean citizens to come to church and learn practical skills such as guitar lessons, flower arranging, travel tips, computer skills, and other useful classes. The culmination of this group's study is the offering of citizenship classes. The Culture Center is under the direction of a retired Korean school principal, Dr. Jung Choi. This former educator came to the United States and received her doctorate in theology from Regents University. She came as a visitor to FBC Duluth in an attempt to discover what was happening at this cross-cultural church. This new offering began a year ago with only six participants; there are now over one hundred.

Many immigrants who move to Duluth come from very Catholic cultures. First Baptist Church quite often is their first non-Catholic religious service. Crossing over to celebratory worship in a multicultural setting is not a difficult leap. However, talking to this group about membership and church involvement is often perceived as forsaking their family traditions and causes pushback and contemplative pause. Some have described leaving the Catholic Church as insulting to family back home, even though attending an evangelical church is their real preference.

Relocation Issues

This leads to the second group of complexities—*relocation issues*. I am writing this chapter in the midst of the 2016 election cycle, and one of the critical stumping issues for candidates is immigration. I never thought during my seminary education in the 1980s that one of my greatest needs would be to immerse myself in immigration law. I have been to immigration court on numerous occasions to assist the members and attenders of

FBCD. A recent article in the *Wall Street Journal* declared our county, Gwinnett County, Georgia, the twenty-fifth largest populace of undocumented immigrants in the entire nation.[30] I am not a lawyer, nor do I claim any expertise on this subject, but after years of dealing with good people attempting to do the right thing, I have made one observation: the system is far too complicated and needs to be simplified!

In an attempt to educate myself on these matters, I have elicited a prayer partnership with a noted immigration attorney in our area, Cornel Potra. We meet every six weeks or so for breakfast and a prayer and share time. Cornel is a native of Romania and an outspoken believer in Jesus Christ. He hosts a local radio program on the largest Hispanic radio station where he gives legal advice over the airways. He has had me as a guest on his program to promote multicultural activities held at our church. Attorney Potra has been a great source of support for me as I have learned the difference between a student visa, a religious worker visa, and a spousal visa. Which visas allow working for income? And are there limitations that need to be watched and checked periodically? This friendship has been a huge blessing in helping me answer some of these questions as I have pursued a multicultural model of ministry.

We have members and attenders at FBCD at various phases of their documentation status. There is a huge need for clearly defined limitations that are purely based on the immigration laws. A police background check is required for service in any of the student areas of our church. Undocumented immigrants are not allowed to serve in these areas due to the inability to secure a clear check on their behalf. In these instances, other areas of service are suggested and fostered.

Recruitment Issues

A third complicated arena regards *recruitment issues*. Over the past five years, we have seen an increasing percentage of new members coming from non-Anglo backgrounds. Yet, many ethnic minorities remained uninvolved in the volunteer ministries of the church. During open dialogue with numerous members of various ethnicities, we discovered that non-Anglo people attending a predominantly Anglo church feel like guests even after becoming members. They do not wish to impose their opinions or their energies where they may not be appreciated or desired. In order to solicit their much-needed participation, a persistent invitation process must be activated.

As people of various ethnicities have begun to see our staff and leadership grow more and more diverse, this process has become much less difficult. However, a concerted effort to secure involvement must continue if we wish to overcome the cultural barrier of investment in ministry. An announcement in the church periodical for "all interested parties" to make themselves known will only further alienate the minority populace of the congregation. And it will wrongly imply to the majority group that there is a lack of desire for shared ministry to take place. Internationals still consider themselves guests as a minority culture in an American church, and many cultures consider it an insult to the host to assume authority or leadership without being recruited to perform such tasks. Many ethnic-minority members are merely waiting for a personal invitation to become involved in the ministry of the church.

Depending on God's Spirit

I am blessed to serve alongside an extraordinary staff and group of lay leaders. But the success of First Baptist Church in transitioning to a multicultural ministry has not been based upon the collective wisdom of our leadership team. The real credit for the phenomenal transformation of our church must accurately be ascribed to a dependence upon God's Spirit for guidance, strength, and encouragement. The Scripture says, "Trust in the LORD with all your heart, and do not rely on your own understanding; think about Him in all your ways, and He will guide you on the right paths" (Prov. 3:5–6).

Recently a ministry student connected to our church was told by the president of a major parachurch organization that the goal of our church is simply "an impossible task." The seasoned minister instructed the naïve student that apart from a movement of the Spirit of God, cultures will never come together in one church setting. The passionate student responded, "Isn't that what we should desire, a movement of the Spirit of God?" There are some situations at FBC Duluth that can only be explained as a fresh movement of the Spirit of God. Here is the account of one such situation that happened the week that I wrote this chapter.

The Sunday after Easter 2016 was also the first weekend for public school spring break in our area. With numerous vacationing families, attendance at the church was about half of the previous week's resurrection celebration. Worship was spirited, yet visibly smaller in number. I was beginning a new sermon series: *The Better Life: Lessons from the Book of Hebrews*. My first sermon was "The Person of the Better Life," a lesson about the ultimate revelation we have in Jesus Christ. As the invitation song commenced, a tall African gentleman came and stood at the altar with head bowed in prayer. I approached him and learned his name—Jude Nathaniel. I asked his purpose in coming to the altar. He responded. "This is my first time to be in this church and the Spirit of the Lord has told me to become a member." Discerning his accent, I inquired his native country. Proudly he proclaimed, "I am from Nigeria." Enthusiastically I responded that I had been in Nigeria the previous August. Jude asked if he could go and reunite with his wife, Susan, who was seated in the rear of the sanctuary caring for their newborn. Susan also desired church membership. A couple visiting for the very first time in the church had been led by the Spirit of God to come and initiate church membership.

I shared the story with the congregation and sent this precious couple to our new members' room, where we process decisions made in the worship service. After the benediction prayer, there is an open invitation for everyone to come and meet my wife and me in our International Grounds Café for the After Party. Before I could even get to the café, I was intercepted in the hallway by a visiting lady. Marina Dakouri is a young mother originally from Ivory Coast, Africa. Her native language is French, but she speaks English well enough to communicate. Marina grabbed me by the arm and said, "I, too, want to become a member." I inquired as to whether she had attended a Christian church in her homeland. She indicated, "I was Catholic, but I desire to know about your faith." To be more thorough in counsel, I made an appointment for my wife and me to visit her home on Monday evening. Later in the day, I learned that her ten-year-old son John had made a similar request in Sunday school the week prior.

The blessings of the day were not complete yet. A third African couple came to the After Party in the café, Robert and Pamela Buziba from Uganda. Robert indicated that they had been attending the church for the past four Sundays, but because they had to hurry to retrieve their two preschoolers from the children's area after church, our paths had never crossed. Robert asked how to initiate the membership process because his family was ready to unite with the fellowship. I made an appointment for Wednesday evening to visit the Buzibas and discuss church membership. Three new families in one day—not bad for one of the lowest attended days of the year!

Monday arrived with the anticipated meeting with Marina Dakouri. Glenda and I entered her apartment and were invited to sit in the living room. John stayed in his room, but little sister Briana acted as co-hostess and as interpreter when Mom's English was insufficient. Marina expressed a desire to have a relationship with God as depicted in the service each Sunday at FBC Duluth. After sharing the gospel, with the aid of my new French interpreter Briana, Marina prayed to invite Jesus into her heart! Through her tears she asked if I would share with her son John. Briana summoned her brother to come and hear a word from the pastor. John was somewhat intimidated at the thought of the pastor desiring a word with him, but after some initial awkwardly shy exchange, he indicated his desire to also pray to receive Christ.

Before we engaged in that prayer, little Briana chimed in with a "Me too, me too, I want to pray!"

The glorious conclusion was that Marina and both her children became Christians! Children in our church that become Christians are tutored by our Director of Children's Ministry Jan Langston in a two-hour class we call "C2C" (Come to Christ). The Dakouri children came to the church building the next morning to take the C2C class and prepare for baptism. Upon completion, Jan came in my office to report that she had never been more assured of two children's genuine conversion. She informed me that Mom and children were waiting outside my office to see if I would be available to baptize them the next Sunday. The date was set and we rejoiced together!

Wednesday of the same week was our appointment with the Buzibas. Glenda and I had met Robert and Pamela for the first time on Sunday morning even though they had been attending for about a month. I asked how they had first learned of First Baptist Church. Robert shared that they had been in the United States for about four months and had searched for a place of worship diligently the entire time. He expressed their frustration at the inability to connect with a local congregation. Their search had become so tedious that the two had decided to go to different churches on Sunday mornings and compare notes of their experiences upon returning home. A month earlier, Pamela had discovered FBCD. On her weekly report back to Robert, she enthusiastically exclaimed, "You have to come there with me next week." He proudly announced to me, "We have been at First Baptist Church Duluth every Sunday since."

I asked Robert the reason why they were so attracted to the church. He simply stated, "We sense God in this place." The conversation turned to their church heritage in their native country of Uganda. I discovered that Pamela came from a Catholic background and Robert was reared in an Anglican church. Neither had heard a gospel presentation on how to be "born again." When I gave them an opportunity to pray to receive Christ, they both responded with a resounding "Yes," then dropped to their knees in the living room awaiting further instructions. After the moving experience of witnessing this precious couple's prayer of conversion, Glenda and I were on a spiritual high! Being conscientious of two preschoolers in the house, we began to say our good-byes for the evening. Robert stopped us and said, "We wanted to make ginger tea for you." We graciously accepted and moved our conversation around the kitchen table.

Dialogue turned to information about their homeland. I learned that Uganda has over thirty tribal dialects, and that Robert and Pamela come from different tribes and, therefore, speak different languages. Their common language is English. "But not American English," Robert pointed out. "British English. There is a difference!" Pamela noted that many people in Uganda know Swahili, the primary language spoken in the larger countries in East Africa. With that revelation, Robert excused himself from the table and went into one of the bedrooms. He returned with a beautiful garment of bright colors with shades of blue and orange accents to give to Glenda. Robert explained that he was holding a *lesu*—referred to as a *kanga* in Swahili—the housedress worn by women in Uganda. Pamela instructed that it was to be worn around the midriff and that women wear it during the day while doing housework and taking care of the children. She clarified that in America we may refer to such a garment as an apron.

Glenda was overwhelmed with the gift and explained that the beauty of the linen appeared to be more suited for Sunday church than for house cleaning! Across the bottom of the garment was a sentence written in an unfamiliar language. Robert shared with glee, "It is Swahili, and it reads 'the love of God has brought us together.' That is why we want you to have it." Glenda was so thankful and genuinely honored by the gift. The love of God had indeed brought the Buzibas into our path.

The week was only halfway over, but I was already so spiritually uplifted that I felt I was walking three feet above the ground! The latter half of the week allowed me ample opportunities to share the glorious stories of the conversion experiences that had taken place on Monday and Wednesday.

A third African family sought to make an appointment with me. Charles Okyere, a gentleman from Ghana, has been attending FBCD for about three years. Charles and his wife, Joyce, have three children: two boys, Terry and Prince, and one daughter, Tracy. Recently Tracy had given birth to their first grandchild, a beautiful baby boy named Elisha. Charles requested that I come and talk with Tracy and the family about our parent/child dedication service. I was a little apprehensive of the meeting because none of the Okyere family had become members of the church to date. Therefore, I had very little information as to their spiritual background.

On Saturday evening, I arrived at the Okyere home. Charles greeted me outside and escorted me in to meet with the family. Joyce was a gracious hostess and asked me to sit in the living room as she called for Tracy to come and meet with me. The new mom came into the room carrying baby Elisha. She allowed me the opportunity to hold him and peer at his beautiful features. Eventually we settled into the purpose of my visit. I explained to Tracy and her parents that the parent/child dedication was a covenant between the church and the family to join together as partners in the spiritual instruction of the child so that in due time, Lord willing, he would come to personal faith in Christ. The trio on the couch nodded in approval and stated their desire to do just that. Charles said that he and Joyce wanted to join the church and they gave clear testimony of their faith.

I looked at Tracy and asked her desire. She said that she prayed often and every Sunday followed me in the "sinner's prayer" at the close of the service, though she really did not fully understand its significance. I began at that point and shared the gospel with this young mother. At the conclusion, Tracy prayed aloud in the presence of her parents to become a follower of Jesus Christ! She was now ready to partner with her church in the spiritual development of her precious child, Elisha. The Okyeres' two sons, Terry and Prince, were not present for this exchange, but both later expressed faith in Christ and were baptized!

The next morning was Sunday and I could not wait to share with the church the phenomenal events of the past week. The service began with the baptism of Marina and her two children, John and Briana. At the invitation time, the Buzibas and the Okyeres came forward to become members of the fellowship. Added to their number was an "all-American" teenager, Cale Majors, who had accepted Christ during our youth discipleship weekend four weeks earlier. He was accompanied by his mother, Misty, who grew up in First Baptist Church but had left as a young adult and now desired to be a part of the fellowship again. This mother/son duo also expressed the leadership of God's Spirit as a decisive factor in the timing of their decision.

There is no systematic explanation for what had transpired in our church. In total, five families from five different countries (Nigeria, Ivory Coast, Uganda, Ghana, and the United States) had come to our church in an eight-day time period. Ten of them were requesting believer's baptism. None of them were connected to each other in any way. And yet each of them had a common theme in explaining their decision to come: "The Spirit of God is directing me to do this." The success of the multicultural church is totally dependent upon the direction of the Spirit of God. Where people are open to being used by Him, the Spirit will exercise power to draw and disciple new believers. He awaits the places that will be faithful to carry the gospel to all nations.

The multicultural path is filled with difficult decisions and plenty of outspoken critics. Indeed, the critics are right. We cannot do this. But the Spirit of God can. The church that learns to depend on God's Spirit will find that He is sufficient to meet every need. The journey to multiculturalism has been a faith-stretching experience both for myself and for our church. Learning to rely upon God's providence for resources and humbly seeking His infinite wisdom have paved the road for maturation and discipleship in our church.

CHAPTER NINE

▼ ▼ ▼

I Had No Idea . . .

The Costs of Multicultural Ministry

*"For which of you, wanting to build a tower, doesn't
first sit down and calculate the cost to see if he has
enough to complete it? Otherwise, after he has laid the
foundation and cannot finish it, all the onlookers will
begin to make fun of him, saying, 'This man started
to build and wasn't able to finish.'" (Luke 14:28–30)*

For years I have enjoyed attending the annual meeting of the
Southern Baptist Convention. This denominational gathering
is part inspiration and part information. The meeting takes place
in a different city each year, allowing my wife, Glenda, and I to
explore some of America's great urban centers. Years ago the
convention was being held in San Antonio, Texas. It was our first
occasion to visit this culturally rich, beautiful, riverfront city. Our
hotel was a short walk from the convention center. We so enjoyed

the stroll down the Riverwalk each evening when the sessions came to a close.

On the last night of the convention meeting we noticed a sandwich board advertisement in our hotel lobby as we left for the session. The posted advertisement read: "Stop by for your choice from the dessert cart with coffee . . . $4.95." The board caught our attention, so Glenda and I said we would immediately return after the night session for a going-away treat. As we made our way back to the hotel that evening, our anticipation grew as to the possible choices from an array of delectable desserts that would soon be our decisive dilemma.

When we arrived at the hotel restaurant, the dining area was packed. Evidently every other conventioneer saw the same advertisement! Glenda and I debated whether the wait would be worth the satisfaction of our sweet cravings. By this time, we had made the event our quest for the evening and felt that we must see it through to conclusion.

The wait was not nearly as long as we anticipated. Soon we were sitting, sipping coffee, and awaiting the opportunity to select from the ravishing choices available at the dessert cart. Our server came by to take our order and we indicated that, like everyone else in the establishment, we had come for the dessert. Then came the devastating word: "We are *out* of desserts."

I questioned the universality of the statement: "You're out of ALL desserts?" Apologetically, the young lady offered her only compromise: "We do have raspberries and ice cream." Not wanting to admit defeat, I instructed her to bring us the sole remaining sweet offering.

Trying not to let the disappointing news upset our last evening in this majestic city, we enjoyed coffee and awaited our
mandated "choice." The wait seemed endless, which was puzzling
considering the no-bake option we were about to receive. At last,
the server reappeared with our order in hand. There were two
individual dishes of vanilla ice cream with approximately two
tablespoons of ice cream in each. Then came a beautiful pyramid
of raspberries, obviously hand-placed in position with each berry
faced downward to expose their plump and colorful nature. Now
I knew the reason for the delay, someone had spent the last thirty
minutes placing each berry in its proper place. Not exactly the
Mississippi mud cake we had anticipated, but an aesthetically
beautiful and new experience nonetheless.

It was difficult to find the heart to dismantle this work of berry
art, but after we each dipped a dozen berries or so into our mini
portion of ice cream, we were ready to receive our check and head
back to the room. I reached for my wallet to pay cash, remember-
ing the $4.95 special. I retrieved a twenty-dollar bill and motioned
for our server. She brought me the check and I handed her the
money without looking at the calculated amount. Looking back
at me with disdain, she informed me that the amount rendered
was insufficient. I took the bill to figure out how this could be.
To my amazement, the amount required was over thirty-six dol-
lars! The coffees were $5 each, ice creams were $5 each, and the
picturesque pyramid of berries was $12. Tax added had brought
the ticket to the alarming new total. When the dessert cart was no
longer available, I should have asked the menu price for the sub-
stitution offered. However, due to this negligence—and the lack

of an attempt to inform me—I was left in the frustrating position of paying for something that was beyond my means.

Counting the Cost: Four Dangers of Multicultural Ministry

This story is true and has been used as a life lesson on numerous occasions throughout my ministry. I place it here because I am aware that many readers of this book will not take the time to consider the cost of moving a church to a multicultural model. Many churches are considering making this move for many different reasons. Some churches have existed for decades and are now seeing the cultural landscape around them change. Others are new churches that are excited about the opportunity to jump into multicultural ministry. Please hear the advice of someone traveling this path currently: There is a price to pay and I do not want you to be caught off guard when the bill is due.

As with any major change, leaders must have a grasp on the situation around them. In a SWOT analysis (Strengths, Weaknesses, Opportunities, Threats), the last step is to analyze potential threats. My desire is to help churches who are considering the shift to multicultural ministry get a grasp on the potential threats and dangers around them. There are four main dangers in the shift to multicultural ministry.

Debt

As I have observed the struggles of local churches in transition, those with debt service accentuate their difficulties exponentially. I have witnessed churches close their doors and sell off facilities due to an inability to perform ministry because of inordinate debt. Many of these congregations were once strong, vibrant testimonies in their local settings. Now, they have been reduced to survival techniques rather than aggressively advancing the cause of Christ.

Debt often realigns priorities and necessitates difficult decisions. We teach our congregants biblical stewardship principles on how to honor God with their resources. The church needs to lead by example in this critical arena, seeking avenues to reduce debt and free up funds for ministry causes.

Discouragement

I once heard a pastor say about a church, "They are prematurely in the past tense." The church lived in the good ol' days with little to no vision of future ministry. Congregants would begin every sentence concerning their church with the phrase "remember when." The past for these types of churches is seldom as glorious as they make it out to be, and their negative attitude becomes a self-fulfilling prophecy. With little to no hope for the future of the fellowship, you can count on little to no future fellowship. When congregants reach this stage, they become a giant billboard to the community that the church has lost its passion to make any real local impact.

Gatherings in churches in this stage are like a pity party, often times exaggerating past accomplishments and never offering constructive answers to current situations. Many have heard the old saying, "misery loves company." This is true! Miserable people surround themselves with other miserable people. No real answers to life's question are given in this toxic environment. If we are content to live in the past instead of moving ahead with boldness, we will never get past the discouragement phase of multicultural ministry.

But there is a flipside to this coin. Even those churches that boldly and courageously move into the arena of multicultural ministry will face serious discouragement. There will be Acts 6 moments when a certain people group comes to your office and tells you they feel left out—left out of leadership, left out of ministry, etc. There will be moments when you receive a letter like the one I discussed in chapter 7. Even for those with the most faith, the most dependence on the Spirit, and the most courage, this walk will, at times, be discouraging.

Disharmony

I want to be brutally honest with anyone considering taking the journey of becoming a multicultural church. People will leave! There will be some passive-aggressive types that will simply slip out the side door of church fellowship without raising any issues. And there will be others who adamantly oppose the process and question the motive of those leading the way. Regardless of how well you handle the shift, *people will leave.* However, in most transitional areas, people were already leaving! They were not only leaving the church, but leaving the area.

Each person leaving a church or area is connected to numerous others who are staying. Lack of consistent contact brings strain to relationships and causes people to wonder what's happening to "my church." Many people are willing to persist through change until it affects their personal relationships. This crisis is a testing ground for whether the individual is making decisions based on

I HAD NO IDEA . . .

comfort or conviction. The multicultural church path will always challenge people's comfort levels and will often be the origin for disharmony.

Demise

Sadly, churches that do not adequately prepare for and adequately respond to the first three dangers will meet the fourth: demise. Failing to embrace and counteract discouragement and disharmony and failing to avoid debt will assure the demise of the church. Churches are asking themselves one of two defining questions. One is proactive—*What must we do to grow in this environment?* The other is reactive—*How do we stop people from leaving the church?* The latter is really a defeated view and is often coupled with improper motivation. I have observed countless churches nostalgically clinging to their past, rather than embracing the present and forging into the future. This good-ol'-days approach is equivalent to hoping the death of the fellowship doesn't occur on their watch. The real strategy is marked by one pathetic question—*How do we die slower?*

On the Offensive

Churches who will succeed in the pursuit of multicultural ministry will not wait to respond to the discouragement and disharmony; they will stay ahead of the game. Churches that are willing to count the cost and commit to the process can thrive in a multicultural setting. Here is how I suggest staying ahead of the downward spiral and following a path to health and spiritual vitality.

Responsible Financial Decisions

Financial health is accomplished by living within budgetary boundaries. However, the church's budget may need adjustment to reflect the new vision of multicultural ministry. This transition will demand critical evaluation of every aspect of ministry—staff needed to accomplish the vision, new ministry offerings that adjust to our changing audience, and prioritization of the things that will most benefit the accomplishment of the vision. These decisions need to be deliberate and targeted to meet needs. The consequences for "no action" can be fatal to the church!

Rejoice in Diversity

Rather than longing for the good ol' days and suffering from the discouragement of a nostalgic longing for the past, our church has learned to embrace and celebrate the opportunities God is bringing to our front door. First Baptist Church Duluth has been recognized as a leader in the multicultural movement. Our church has been featured in newspaper articles in the *Wall Street Journal*, the *Christian Index*, and our local newspaper, the *Gwinnett Daily Post*. Our story has been recounted in the *Atlanta* magazine and LifeWay's *Facts and Trends*. I have been privileged to be interviewed on *Life with Purpose Radio* and *Church Answers with Thom Rainer*. The church has recognized that our influence is truly global in nature. Over the past five years, people from forty different countries have become members at FBCD. Some have left and returned to their homeland, taking with them the rich experience of being a part of a multicultural ministry. Our church is celebrating a global impact on every Sunday in every worship service.

Because we have embraced our changing community, we have set an example for community cooperation, allowing us to become a leading voice for constructive change. We have become active partners with city officials in understanding how better to serve this diverse community and bring people together across cultural lines. Our current local campaign, #withduluth, is enabling our church to connect with the community by enlisting members as volunteers in city-wide events and services.

This unique approach is a new paradigm for ministry and, therefore, is setting new standards for measuring success. Our church does not have the same attendance numbers that it had fifteen years ago, but we are accomplishing more in every aspect of our local community than ever before in the history of the church. Moreover, we are planting churches among different people groups in international settings for the first time! Our success is measured in global and local impact.

Be Relational

The death cycle takes a church into disharmony. In Acts 6, the first deacons were selected for the purpose of protecting the fellowship against racial disharmony. The early church was growing so rapidly that there arose a dispute as to whether non-Jews were receiving equal treatment as their Jewish brothers and sisters. Equality and fairness across cultural lines was the reason behind the election of the initial deacon body. In that vein, I have attempted to keep our leaders mindful of their God-given responsibility to guard against disruptive forces. One of the key elements of establishing the basis of cooperation is a clear and concise vision communicated by the leadership. With this in mind, I have set out to garner the support and cooperation of key leaders within the fellowship. God has gifted us with men and women that are respected leaders in their fields. I have sought business advice from economists, personnel advice from human resource managers, and visionary guidance from entrepreneurs.

Every church, regardless of size, has a group of key influencers within the fellowship. The church seldom makes any significant decisions without the advocacy of this unofficial team. Some rise to this standing within the church by longevity of membership, and others receive this respect by aiding the church in previous crisis decisions. For the most part, leaders will simply rise to the level of influence. Every pastor desiring to be a change agent needs to accurately identify this group of leaders within the church and spend quality time discipling them and explaining the vision of multicultural ministry to them. Responsible people desiring the best for their church will respond to leadership that includes them in the process. At First Baptist Church Duluth, this influential group created a web of peer connections that provided an organic communication of multicultural ministry data and answered questions arising from the church body. Failure to concur at this level should cause tremendous pause, allowing the opportunity to reevaluate processes and the message of how to illicit the support of the masses. The key is to remain patient and do the necessary work with this group, assuring success while dispelling fears within the body.

Many times I have requested personal support and endorsement of ideas from these leaders, realizing that their spheres of influence collectively will always exceed mine personally. Having strong supportive leadership has been instrumental in our church's successful transition to date. As fellowship flare-ups have occurred (and they will), deacons and committee leaders have been quick to respond and grant renewed commitment to the vision of our purposeful path. Due to the shared process in formation of the vision, staying the course has been a joint effort with relatively few dissenters among the core of leadership. The congregation takes their cues from an effective leadership team. When the church sees a group of leaders that are all-in on a concept, they usually want to follow.

Early in our transition process the deacons of FBC Duluth took ownership of modeling cross-cultural relationships. In a meeting that I missed because of family vacation, the deacon chair challenged our deacons to identify leaders within the congregation from different cultural backgrounds. The goal was to form relationships that would lead to diversification in our leadership body. I returned from vacation to learn of this process and glorified God that our church was headed in this direction! Since that fateful meeting we have elected seven men to serve as deacons from non-Anglo backgrounds. This diversification has spilled over into every area of church leadership.

As I have observed the heightened attention in our country to racial conflict and prejudicial treatment, I have become increasingly convinced that the church is to be the catalyst for authentic change. When the church of Jesus Christ gets leaders from different backgrounds to lay aside differences and unite around the common message of redemption, the community can't help but notice. We believe with all sincerity that First Baptist Church Duluth holds the key to the complicated and controversial issues that come with living in a majority-minority city.

Be Relevant

There are all kinds of symptoms of a dying church, but there is one primary cause for demise—losing relevance in the local community. Scattered across metro Atlanta are church buildings that once were filled with congregants being nourished with God's truth. Now, they are in various stages of deterioration due to lack of funds because of dwindling church attendance. What caused this plight on our city's spiritual landscape? It was the inability to remain relevant in a changing environment.

I once heard this phenomenon referred to as "the frog in a kettle." This descriptive analogy is that when you place a live frog in a vat of warm water it will not jump out. The warm-blooded animal enjoys its surroundings and soaks in the soup. If the temperature is increased incrementally, the frog will not react, eventually being boiled alive by virtue of its failure to respond. In case study upon case study, churches in our locale failed to recognize the changing environment around them, ultimately leading to the demise of their congregations.

The first step to becoming relevant is becoming a student of one's changing community. Our area is changing so rapidly that it is difficult to keep up with the data. When I first moved to Duluth, the fastest growing people group was Korean immigrants. I pass a dozen Korean congregations on the commute between my home and FBC Duluth. More recently, there has been a large influx of South Asian people from India and Pakistan. A new Hindu temple has been constructed less than a mile from our church. There is also a rapidly growing African community. In 2015, we had four families come to First Baptist Church Duluth from Nigeria. This week, as I write this chapter, we have added new families from

Nigeria, Ivory Coast, and Uganda to our fellowship. Our changing community continues to be a radical case study.

Once one comprehends the change taking place within a community, one must seek expertise in understanding new cultures that populate that area. International missionaries have referred to this process as locating the "person of peace" within the new culture, based on the words of Jesus in Luke 10:5–6. This person may not yet be a Christian, but is nonetheless willing to share key cultural information that will aid in presenting the gospel. God has provided numerous persons of peace in my path to enhance my understanding of cross-cultural relationships. Often this began within my prayer life, asking for God to send me someone of a particular people group who would be a champion in helping me reach their native people. These person-of-peace relationships may begin as a simple friendship and evolve into a full-blown ministry partnership.

A third step in becoming relevant is being a visible advocate of community leaders. We found that the same issues facing our church were happening in every arena of community living. Therefore, we wanted to clearly communicate our support for our city government by being one of the sponsors of the mayor's state of the city address. We desired to show support for our local school system by providing a teacher appreciation brunch on faculty work days and taking on volunteer roles in schools to relieve parents and allow them to enjoy their child's program or sports activity.

Churches are often seen more for what they are *against* than what they are *for*, but FBC Duluth has a desire to be *for* our city. In supporting community leaders and initiatives in Duluth, we can be seen as a helpful change agent in our city. This mind-set can be seen in the prophet Jeremiah's words to God's people about how to live as exiles in Babylon:

> This is what the LORD of Hosts, the God of Israel, says to all the exiles I deported from Jerusalem to Babylon: "Build houses and live in them. Plant gardens and eat their produce. Take wives and have sons and daughters. Take wives for your sons and give your daughters to men in marriage so that they may bear sons and daughters. Multiply there; do not decrease. Seek the welfare of the city I have deported you to. Pray to the LORD on its behalf, for when it has prosperity, you will prosper." (Jer. 29:7)

God doesn't want us to be *against* our cities but to be *for* them, partnering with city leaders and working for the welfare of those around us. I told our leadership team that we will know we are experiencing success when they begin seeking us out for the answers to community issues.

By God's grace, we have seen this process begin to happen. No-strings-attached service is recognized and appreciated. I once heard a conference speaker ask, "If your church ceased to exist this week, other than your members, who would notice?" That mental exercise has been a highly motivating part of our efforts and I can share with joy that there would be many in Duluth that would feel a void if FBCD ceased to exist. That mutually caring relationship keeps a church relevant and pays the price for continued ministry impact for the community.

To talk about what relevance is, however, we must talk about what relevance is *not*. Too many churches have capitulated on serious issues in an attempt to be "relevant." Relevance is not submitting to the new sexual norms of the culture. Relevance is not watering down the gospel. Relevance does not mean letting the rock band perform for an hour on Sunday morning and squeezing in a ten-minute "conversation" about a vague, Christian-sounding topic with a couple of Bible verses pulled out of context. In order to be relevant, we must remember that the most relevant thing to every person of every ethnicity in every city for all time is the gospel of Jesus Christ.

Many churches, in the effort to be relevant, have focused on creating a gospel culture apart from gospel truth. This destroys our ability to be in the world but not of the world, and welcomes the world into our pulpits. On the other hand, many churches have hoped to maintain gospel truth with no regard for a gospel culture. This preaches to the world a gospel of condemnation, rather than a gospel of love, which is really no gospel at all. True relevance is preaching gospel truth and embracing a gospel culture; it rejoices in diversity and works for the welfare of its city.

A pyramid of raspberries taught me the importance of counting the cost in a timely manner. Many churches wait too late in the death cycle for adequate transition to meet the needs of their changing community. Insufficient financial resources and a depleted volunteer base accelerate the demise. Often the move to a multicultural model is perceived as an act of desperation to avoid the imminent death of the fellowship. Failure to foresee the cost of transition lulls the congregation into this terminal situation.

Avoiding death is seldom a good motivation. The ever-chang-
ing face of a community can ascertain the difference between a
compassionate motive and a self-serving act of desperation. In
previous chapters, it has been noted that the path to multicultural ministry is deeply rooted in biblical integrity. Counting the
cost of making the difficult accompanying decisions is a practical
exercise required for people taking the journey. Know the cost of
your pyramid of raspberries before you embark on this adventure!

CHAPTER TEN

▼ ▼ ▼

Who's On Board?

The Consumers of Multicultural Ministry

*Come and listen, all who fear God, and I will tell
you what He has done for me. (Psalm 66:16)*

F amous American humorist Mark Twain is attributed with saying, "There is nothing so annoying as a good example." For
those still not convinced of the veracity and viability of a multicultural ministry, I wish to share a good example. This chapter
is a collection of testimonials from people who have joined First
Baptist Church during the previous five years of transition. This
cross section includes people from five different continents. Read
their stories and take note of what attracted them to this unique
ministry and how God called each of them to become a part of
the First Baptist Church Duluth journey.

Name: Babatunde (Bab) and Olufunsho (Olu) Adewoye
Country of Origin: Nigeria
Native Language: Yoruba
Year Joined First Baptist Church Duluth: 2014

First Baptist Church can be described as "heaven on earth," where people from different nations get together every Sunday to give God His food—praises! It is good for people of like minds, regardless of color, race, or sex, to gather and worship God. The wish of the Father is that there be no segregation. The Scripture says, "There is neither Jew nor Greek, there is neither slave nor free man, there is neither male nor female; for all you are one in Christ Jesus" (Gal. 3:28). The First Baptist Church of Duluth has achieved this feat in the present dispensation and it is still ongoing!

My first Sunday in the church revealed the kind of church FBCD is and the kind of pastor who is in charge. At the end of the service there is a welcome reception for first-time visitors hosted by the pastor and his wife. The pastor invited me to his home that week to participate in an ongoing course called "The Multi-Ethnic Christian Life Primer." This invitation was a rare situation compared to my previous church experience. I became convinced in my spirit that this pastor must have the gift of discernment or perhaps he had done a spiritual background check on me.

As I continued to attend the church, I learned that the various nations represented at the church were not just "bench warmers"; they were each given adequate avenues to participate in the worship service. I vividly remember the 2015 Easter Sunday service. The simple phrase "Jesus has risen!" was shared in a variety of different languages—including my native Yoruba—expressing a perfect representation of the worshiping family at the church. Foreigners' involvement of this nature enhances our sense of belonging, and for me personally it has uprooted the "bondage of worship" that had been growing in my heart since coming to America.

Now, I serve as a church usher and a Sunday school volunteer for the four- and five-year-olds. I foresee a church whose tendencies will spread, penetrate, and influence the nations of the world. The pastor has visited my country, Nigeria. He has been in my state and done work among my tribe to establish mission partnership. This is a headquarters of multicultural missions in the making! It is my earnest prayer that the multicultural ministry of First Baptist Church will thrive until the coming of our Savior. AMEN!

Name: HyounKyoung (Grace) Park
Country of Origin: South Korea
Native Language: Korean
Year Joined First Baptist Church Duluth: 2015

First, I would like to thank and praise our Lord who led me to First Baptist Church Duluth! I had been praying that I would not have to move any more to follow a job, but rather would be able to settle where I could serve Him. Whenever I move, I attend a church near my place—mainly Baptist churches and typically Caucasian congregations. But I always felt like a stranger in those churches. I do not mean to say that they were bad churches, but I was curious as to why I would always feel so alone in the Lord's house. My focus had always been to worship the Lord at His house, so I didn't let this lonely feeling bother me. It really did not matter to me until I found First Baptist Church.

After moving to Duluth, I once again searched for a church near my place. I googled churches near my location and FBCD was the first on the list. For some reason I did not feel very attracted to the church, but for whatever reason, when Sunday came, I put the address in my GPS and headed to worship. Later, I found that there are many churches much closer to my place than FBCD. I know God led me to this church!

I still do not know how to explain my experience. When I entered the sanctuary to attend the service, I was overwhelmed by the presence of the Holy Spirit. As Pastor Hearn preached the sermon, I felt tears start in my eyes. These were tears of joy, for I knew that this was the church I had been praying for.

This was not the only reason I was attracted to FBCD. The very next day I attended a Bible study at Pastor Hearn's house. There I discovered his passion for international ministry, especially to reach the various ethnic groups of Duluth. Frankly speaking, I have never seen a church in the United States that embraces different ethnic groups as FBCD does. I have heard many pastors talk about the importance of reaching different groups, yet few seem to make much effort to do so. I sense my pastor's passion and ministry efforts to reach ethnic minorities and have seen this spread throughout the congregation. I have seen and feel the difference in the interaction of the members with each other. They really do care about each other! I believe and pray that God will use this ministry to become a role model for other churches to share God's message and follow His commandments. Praise the Lord! And thank you, Pastor!

Name: Scott and Ginger Hales
Country of Origin: U.S.A.
Native Language: English
Year Joined First Baptist Church Duluth: 2014

We have been members of First Baptist Church Duluth for a little more than a year after transitioning from our previous church, where we had been members for twenty-five years. A multicultural church is not what we were looking for and was not what drew us to the church. We were drawn by the people who immediately reached out to us and welcomed us. We loved the music and the presence of the Holy Spirit during worship. We quickly grew to respect Dr. Hearn as a mission-minded pastor who lives what he preaches and is highly visible in various activities.

We joined without knowing much about the multicultural vision Dr. Hearn has, yet we knew this to be a church that is following the will of God. One Sunday during Communion, the message was translated into four languages for everyone in the service to hear. While I did not understand one word of Korean, Spanish, or Gujarati (an Indian dialect), I did understand that the message was the same, no matter what language was spoken. We all worship the same God!

After joining the church, we attended a new members' class led by our associate pastor along with a Korean ministry intern, Pastor Tom Rhe, and his wife, Cindy. We quickly became good friends with the Rhe family. We have lived in Duluth for fifteen years and this was the first minority family we had ever become friends with. My question is: Why? Why had we not crossed this bridge earlier?

While participating in one of the church's cross-cultural small groups, our eyes were opened. One of the most memorable things said was that eleven o'clock on Sunday is the most segregated hour in America. How could this be? One of the primary messages of Sunday morning is "love your neighbor." How ironic that the same church parking lot used on Friday night football games that attracts all cultures, could be used on Sunday morning to service a monocultural church service. This was a reaffirming moment that Dr. Hearn's vision is the direct will of God for our church. God is the God of ALL people.

Heaven will be filled with individuals from all people groups who believe that Jesus Christ is the Son of God who came to save us. It all boils down to the Great Commandment: Love your neighbor. Our neighbors happen to be very diverse and it has been a blessing to worship and learn side by side.

Name: Verdi N. and Esthela Avila
Country of Origin: Ecuador
Native Languagè: Spanish
Year Joined First Baptist Church Duluth: 2010

For several decades, my wife, Esthela, and I worshipped in Spanish-speaking churches in New York and New Jersey. Upon the birth of our first granddaughter, we moved to Georgia to help out with the family. We began our search for a church among the Spanish-speaking congregations in the Atlanta area. We decided to visit an English-speaking church and found the service and message more to our style of worship. We became members of that church and actively participated in the ministries offered. In time, we moved to Duluth and visited the First Baptist Church. The church was in a transition of leadership, searching for a new senior pastor.

Upon our first visit to First Baptist Church Duluth, we experienced a friendly congregation. The minister of adult education gave us a brief overview of the church and its ministries. When Dr. Hearn was called as pastor, we returned for another visit and attended a Sunday school class. We were immediately welcomed like family. They embraced our ethnicity and invited us to lunch to "break bread" with them after the service. We were invited to a class BBQ dinner the next day. We had never experienced such friendliness and acceptance. We listened attentively as Dr. Hearn delivered his messages and found him to be on point. We were now seriously considering joining the congregation. Scanning the sanctuary each Sunday, I began noticing members of different ethnicities and countries. For me, this was a message that FBCD is a welcoming church for all of God's family. After a few more visits, we decided to become members!

My wife and I became involved in several ministries and participated in the outreach efforts to the large multiethnic community surrounding the church. The existing ethnic diversity of the church was minimal, so we wanted to aid in its increase. Another thing we liked about the church was how welcoming the members were to visitors and to fellow members. This displays true Christian love. FBC Duluth called a Spanish-speaking missionary to do outreach to the local community. Esthela and I became involved in this outreach. Additionally, I observed the church making concerted efforts to reach out to the Indian and Korean communities. Dr. Hearn began a multicultural course, taught in his home, to help members to become cognizant of the cultures around us. Esthela and I participated in the very first course. Now, this is an ongoing offering for our church family.

Additionally, the church has begun to honor other cultures by celebrating their holidays. First Baptist Church Duluth is truly a congregation of members who love Christ and our diversity shouts it for all to hear![31]

Name: Seung-hee (Cindy) and Jeong- doo (Tom) Rhe
Country of Origin: South Korea
Native Language: Korean
Year Joined First Baptist Church Duluth: 2014

I came to First Baptist Church Duluth alongside my husband, Tom Rhe, who is a student at New Orleans Baptist Theological Seminary. Tom is serving as FBCD's first ministry intern bridging relationships with the Korean community, and I serve as the church's first Korean interpreter. God brought us here ready to be used by Him and He equipped us through many types of training beforehand. First Baptist Church Duluth is in many ways like the mission fields that I have served in previously, reaching out to diverse nations with people from the same international background. I am thrilled to be a part of this church. I greatly enjoy the love of the church family, but more than that, my husband and I are doing exactly what we have been gifted by God to do. It is an amazing feeling to be where you are called to be!

To date I have three homes: Korea, where I was born and raised; the *Logos II*, a ministry ship operated by Operation Mobilization traveling on mission to countries throughout the world; and America, my new home, because of the FBCD family. This church means so much to me. I love my church! It bears the fruit of my life.

I once thought that only God knows the genuine heart of a church, whether its members truly desire to reach a diverse community with the gospel of Christ. However, I now strongly believe that God loves FBCD and is very pleased with what we are attempting to do. I am more than ever compelled to pray for the continuance of this wonderful ministry until Jesus comes again. I see God at work through the people of this church as He gathers them from every nation. God will finish what He has begun. We are to be obedient as His workmen. I am filled with joy as I serve at the church, because I believe God cherishes the work of this congregation. I thank God that my husband, Tom, and I, along with our three sons, Joseph, Joel, and Daniel, found this church.[32]

Name: Jackie and Lenny Montalto
Country of Origin: United States
Native Language: English
Year Joined First Baptist Church Duluth: 2013

I (Jackie) have always been looking for a church—not so much for my husband, Lenny. When we relocated to Georgia with Lenny's job, we left family and friends behind. This was a transitional time at work for Lenny and I saw him struggling. One day I stumbled upon a Christian radio station. I would play this station during our commute into work each morning, hoping he would hear something that would soothe him and set the tone for his day. Although it was not an immediate transition, seeds were sown. On our commute, we would drive past all the different denominations of churches on Highway 120 in Duluth. I would imagine one day visiting one of these churches. And one day, we did just that.

I told Lenny that when we feel God's presence, we will know we have found our church. Lenny received a promotion at work and we purchased a house in the area. I began to tell Lenny that we needed to find a church and let God know how thankful we are for the blessings coming our way. When we stepped into First Baptist Church Duluth, our lives totally changed. Smiling faces greeted us, welcomed us, and made us feel like family. I noticed people in the congregation from every generation. Once in the sanctuary, I saw the walls lined with flags from many nations. Lenny and I wondered about the meaning of the display. Pastor Mark Hearn explained during the worship service that the flags represent the birth nations of the members of the church. Since that first day at church, we have watched additional flags go up as new members have joined.

As we continued to get to know the church, we noticed interpreters provided to make the internationals feel welcome. Borrow a set of headphones and hear the service in your own home language . . . WOW! We also observed the church celebrating Indian Independence Day (August 15), Three Kings Day (a Hispanic Christmas tradition on January 6), and Korean/Chinese New Year.

We moved to Georgia from New York, the melting pot of nationalities. Now, we were seeing it in our new church. We felt the Lord's presence inside the church that first day. We knew we had found our church among this gathering of God's people of every color. We asked ourselves, "How could we *not* fit in?" We will soon celebrate two years since we followed Christ and were both baptized at FBCD. God has now led me to be the coordinator for a church-sponsored after-school children's ministry at an elementary school in our community called The Good News Club. Lenny is now playing guitar in the church worship team. We are not only members of the church, we are family! Of all the friends we have had across the years, we never before felt like family—until we came to FBCD. Praise God!

Name: Silvia Mindrescu Rosario and Fernando Rosario
Country of Origin: Silvia—Moldova; Fernando—
      Dominican Republic
Native Language: Silvia—Romanian; Fernando—Spanish
Year Joined First Baptist Church Duluth: 2015

Our family is very unique. We are not only a multilingual family, but also a multinational one. We had been praying and searching for a home church where, along with our children, we could serve and grow spiritually. On a Sunday morning in the summer of 2015, we visited the First Baptist Church of Duluth. Upon our arrival, we were kindly greeted and escorted to the preschool area to register our children for Sunday school.

We requested that our children be placed in the same age-graded class, even though one is in pre-kindergarten and the other is in first grade. This parental decision was to allow our children the opportunity to adapt to their new environment together. Changes are very difficult for my son due to his high-functioning autism. Our children enjoy being in Sunday school classes and look forward weekly to learning more about God and His Word.

Fernando and I were invited to participate in a Bible study class for young married couples. We have been thrilled to study God's Word alongside this incredible group of people. There are many opportunities provided to serve in our church and the community with the gifts God has given us. First Baptist Church is opening its wings to the needs of the international community and more people are being drawn to serve the Lord together! God's presence is REAL here! And He works for the good of those who love Him!

Name: Jazmin Flores and Roberto Vanoye
Country of Origin: Mexico
Native Language: Spanish
Year Joined First Baptist Church Duluth: 2012

The Lord brought us to First Baptist Church Duluth. Coming to an English-speaking church was not our original plan, but God has richly blessed our family's decision to be here. When we first visited the church, we were immediately drawn to the beautiful praise and worship music that drew us closer to God. The warm welcome we received at Sunday school as we enrolled our little ones was priceless. To top things off that morning, Pastor Mark's sermon was spiritually uplifting and just what we needed that day! After church, we attended the reception for newcomers to come and meet Pastor Mark and his wife, Glenda. They presented us a gift bag from the church and thanked us for coming to worship that morning.

As we got to know Pastor Mark, we learned of his heart for multicultural ministry. We believe that it is in keeping with the Great Commission (Matt. 28:19–20). As we involved ourselves in the church's ministry, I (Jazmin) became active in women's ministry. This has been an effective tool for witnessing to the Duluth community. Soon I was helping in planning and implementation of wonderful activities. This group of ladies embraced me and always made me feel at home.

I believe that First Baptist Church will reach Duluth with the gospel, because my church shows no distinctions. Every people group from every language is welcome here![33]

Name: SoYoung and K. J. Lee
Country of Origin: South Korea
Native Language: Korean
Year Joined First Baptist Church Duluth: 2014

I remember my first conversation with Pastor Mark. We had a conversation with great gravity. He portrayed an extraordinary desire to reach out to various people groups in the Duluth community. When he invited me, a first-generation Korean, to be a part of the church staff, I saw how cultural and ethnic differences could be overcome by God's Spirit and a heart to worship the Lord as one body of Christ. The vision and passion of FBCD is to radically follow God's will and embrace all people, cultures, and ethnicities. This vision ignited in my heart and captivated me. This new staff role was to be more than just a ministry position for me; it was a new home for continued growth in my relationship with Christ.

I serve as the director of preschool ministries at FBCD. I have observed people enter though the church doors from a variety of backgrounds. God has been developing in me a compassionate heart like Jesus and a bold, willing spirit to fulfill His Great Commission. I have seen those who come under the wings of my church be touched by the genuine love of the people and their warm-hearted care. As our church continues to seek unity and oneness of spirit, I envision the congregation's unrestricted love shining the light of gospel into the hearts of many. "May they be brought to complete unity to let the world know that you sent me and have loved them even as you have loved me" (John 17:23).[34]

Name: Kadmiel and Isoleth Kumar
Country of Origin: Kadmiel—India; Isoleth—El Salvador
Native Language: Kadmiel—Sambalpuri; Isoleth—Spanish
Year Joined First Baptist Church Duluth: 2012

Isoleth and I recently had the opportunity to serve one of our Sunday morning preschool classes. There were three two-year-olds in attendance that day: Isaac—a blonde, Caucasian boy; David, whose parents are from Mexico; and Abigail, whose parents are from Nigeria. Halfway through the lesson, a new church attender from Brazil named Eude walked into class with his beautiful three-year-old daughter, Elisa. Later that morning, our church Preschool Director SoYoung Lee, a native of Korea, stopped by to check on our class progress. Seven total adults and children passed through the classroom that morning and they represented seven different nations: Mexico, Nigeria,

South Korea, Brazil, El Salvador, India, and the United States. By the way, the worker in the room next to ours caring for the bed babies stopped in to see if we needed help—she is from Ethiopia! So make it eight! What a beautiful illustration of First Baptist Church Duluth!

Five years ago I met Pastor Mark through my brother Daniel Kumar, who serves as a pastor in New Delhi, India. My wife, Isoleth, and I were looking for a church with a heart for missions. We wanted a church that reaches out to other nations as well as the various ethnic groups living next door to us. We were very frustrated in our inability to find a local church that was making any concerted effort to reach out to the thriving South Asian community of Greater Atlanta. In our first meeting, Pastor Mark challenged me to consider that if I was convicted in my spirit of this neglect, perhaps I was being called to do something about it! With the support of Pastor Mark and a host of FBCD volunteers, we were able to organize two outreach events among the South Asian community in Gwinnett County.

During our meeting, Pastor Mark told Isoleth and me about the more than fifty language groups in the Duluth school system. When we first visited the church, we observed the flags of different countries on display, we were warmly welcomed, and we immediately knew this was going to be our new home. At First Baptist Church, we do not ignore ethnic and cultural differences; we embrace them. We have appreciated our church celebrating Indian Independence Day and *El dia de los Reyes* (The Day of the Kings), as well as the Fourth of July. Everyone has great fun! Our church is gradually attracting more and more people from diverse backgrounds. We are beginning to reflect the local community. I

am proud to be a part of First Baptist Church Duluth and blessed
to have Dr. Mark Hearn as my pastor and spiritual leader.[35]

Conclusion

These stories are a sampling of the incredible people God is
directing to our community and gathering at First Baptist Church
Duluth. These testimonials come from ten households, representing nine countries and six language groups. Yet, this diverse
group worships in the same setting and serves the community as a
united ministry team. Their backgrounds are obviously extremely
different. However, there are common elements that appear in
each of their stories. Here are three for you to consider.

A Place of Inclusion

You may have noticed that each family indicated an immediate sense of *belonging* when worshiping at FBCD. This spirit of
inclusion is fostered and encouraged. The flags in the sanctuary provide an immediate impression that there is something
different about the makeup of this body of believers. Almost
every Christian church claims to be a "friendly church." Quite
obviously, not all churches can claim that mantle with integrity.
However, crossing cultural and often language barriers requires
that a congregation have a heightened awareness of the need to
be hospitable.

A Place of Intentionality

One of the great things to witness at FBCD is the cross-
cultural experience—observing Koreans participating in the

Spanish Three Kings Day celebration, or Chinese families attending high tea for Indian Independence Day. I have observed that deference to *any* minority culture endears *all* minority cultures to the humble spirit that is exhibited. We will by all probability never be able to offer our worship services in all of the fifty-seven identified language groups that comprise our local community. The fact that we are currently offering our services with live interpretation to the two largest language groups in our area indicates to every language group our heart for international people.

A Place of Intangibles

The presence of God's Spirit cannot be programmed or predicted. The Bible clearly teaches that God blesses the practices that honor Him and have lasting Kingdom value. These ten families have individually indicated the blessings of God upon this ministry. At First Baptist Church, we do not want to take this for granted. God is bringing the nations to our doorstep for a purpose. We are embracing this phenomenon and giving praise, honor, and glory to the Almighty. May God bless us with hundreds more families that will aid in the work of reaching the nations among us!

▼ ▼ ▼

Is the Sky Falling?

The Crisis of Multicultural Ministry

The account you have just read is a journey that is still in progress. Therefore, there is not a neat and tidy ending to this book, but a word of both encouragement and warning. A church that enters the path to multicultural competence is going to find both uphill battles and exhilarating rewards. This journey has not merely been a corporate endeavor, but also a profound and life-altering path for me personally; it has changed some of my core conceptions of ministry.

I mentioned previously that my educational preparation for ministry included a bachelor's degree in biblical studies, a master's degree in evangelism, and a doctorate in the field of church growth. My entire ministry has been a practicum on how to grow the church numerically. In my studies, I read all the leaders of the church growth movement. Included in my study were the writings of Donald McGavran, considered by many the founder of the modern-day church growth movement. McGavran (1897–1990) was a third-generation missionary to India who later became the first dean of the Institute for Church Growth at Fuller Theological Seminary in Pasadena, California.

McGavran's life work was to discover practices that would enhance the spread of the gospel to every people group on the planet. In 1955 he published his most definitive work, *The Bridges of God*. This book is most noted as the beginning of the teaching of the homogeneous unit principle (HUP), a concept he later expanded upon in his work *Understanding Church Growth* (1970). McGavran explains that people "like to become Christians without crossing racial, linguistic, or class barriers."[36] This principle became the driving force of a generation of theological training.

Megachurches sprouted across the American landscape in the 1980s and '90s using the HUP (homogeneous unit principle). Demographic studies of potential church start areas determined not only the race and predominant language group of the area, but also could identify the preferred style of music and political leanings of future attendees. The science of this movement was flawless. I was not only an advocate of this principle, but also a practitioner and a teacher. I have had the privilege of being an adjunct faculty member at two different institutions, teaching evangelism and discipleship at the undergraduate level. One of these opportunities was at Crossroads Bible College in Indianapolis, Indiana, a school designed to teach young ministers how to impact urban centers with the gospel message. I leaned on my experience and training and regretfully taught the HUP to eager college students seeking ministry advice and mentoring. Since being immersed in a rapidly diversifying community, I have learned the need for cross-cultural interaction and the blessing that comes when all congregants do *not* come from similar backgrounds.

I want to clearly state I believe that the HUP does work as an effective tool for evangelism. Many of today's megachurches are bright examples of consumer-based results that if you provide what people desire, they will come. However, I have become convinced that the HUP has been misused as an excuse for continuing the segregation of churches to prioritize comfort above Christian influence. I believe in the value of language churches to provide a needed acclamation to our predominantly English-speaking society. However, as the second generation enters the scene, a more integrated approach is needed to maximize community impact. We at FBCD use the HUP as it was originally intended—as an evangelistic strategy. People are attracted to the gospel more commonly when presented in their native tongue by someone from a similar cultural background. For this reason, we have Bible studies in Spanish and Korean. People of different cultural backgrounds assist in the after-church "meet and greet," allowing an immediate connection to the church body. However, we at FBCD worship together as one body. This journey has made me examine my theological formation to determine if it is based upon biblical truth or merely comfort and convenience.

The multicultural church movement in America is a relatively new phenomenon. Sociologists Korie Edwards, Brad Christerson, and Michael Emerson published a study in 2013 in the *Annual Review of Sociology,* defining a multicultural church as a congregation with a least 20 percent of attendees being from a people group other than the majority culture. This "tipping point" by sociological standards provides necessary opportunities for intercultural associations. When at least 20 percent of the church is of diverse culture, there is a 99 percent probability of random interaction across cultural lines. Based upon this definition for a multicultural congregation, 7.7 percent of all churches in America were deemed multicultural in 1998. However, by the year 2010, the number of multicultural churches had risen to 13.7 percent, an impressive increase of over 75 percent. Sociologists are predicting a seismic wave as multicultural churches become the norm rather than the exception in American cities.[37]

Mark DeYmaz describes the changing landscape among American churches as a multicultural church movement. He describes the current status as "Pioneer Stage." He points out that "pioneers are usually not the first people to discover things. More typically they are the first to recognize the intrinsic value and significance of something."[38] I am proud to be identified as a pioneer in this movement. But, the pioneer phase is quickly yielding to the "Early Adopter Stage." DeYmaz predicts the ushering in of this phase by the turn of the decade, when estimates indicate that 20 percent of American churches will have reached the identifiable 20 percent threshold. At this pace, multicultural churches will reach the "Mainstream Stage," with over 50 percent of churches recognizably diverse by the year 2050![39]

As the cities of America become more visibly diverse, so too must the churches that are taking the gospel to those cities. I have lamented as I have observed the demise of many inner-city congregations in my denomination due to the failure to remain relevant in their local setting as cultural changes overtook their region. The study conducted by Edwards, Christerson, and Emerson notes that one of the primary predictors of a congregation's ability to make the change to a multicultural model is to intentionally and routinely promote diversity.[40] Success is not measured solely by numerical data but by faithfulness to the calling and adherence to the cause.

The motivation for becoming a multicultural church cannot be political correctness. I have read a quote attributed to multiple sources that says, "Change occurs when the pain of staying the same exceeds the pain of change." This may be true, but alleviation of pain is a lousy motivation! This cannot be merely a rescue option for a dying church in a changing community. The motivation needs to be the compelling call of the Great Commission to take the gospel to every people group without exclusion! The crisis in my journey caused me to examine my motivation and lead the church I serve on a path to be impactful in our local community, by being an example of what heaven will be for all people. Faithfulness to the command of God's call is the only genuine motivation for the pursuit of the multicultural church. Only by this motivation can we truly experience church in technicolor.

> *After this I looked, and there was a vast multitude from every nation, tribe, and language, which no one could number, standing before the throne and before the Lamb. They were robed in white and palm branches in their hands. And they cried out in a loud voice: Salvation belongs to our God, who is seated on the throne, and to the Lamb! (Revelation 7:9–10)*

APPENDIX A

▼ ▼ ▼

Flags on Display in the Worship Center

Argentina
Bahamas
Brazil
Cameroon
Canada
China
Cuba
Dominican Republic
Ecuador
Egypt
El Salvador
Ethiopia
Ghana

Great Britain
Guyana
Haiti
Hungary
India
Indonesia
Italy
Ivory Coast
Jamaica
Lebanon
Liberia
Lithuania
Mexico

Moldova	South Vietnam
Myanmar	St. Kitts/Nevis
Nigeria	Taiwan
Peru	Thailand
Republic of Benin	Uganda
Russia	United States
South Korea	Venezuela

Flags of members and regular attenders since tracking this data in 2012.

▼ ▼ ▼

First Baptist Church Duluth Vision Frame

Mission (What we do)

To be a united community of faith that loves, reaches, and disciples all people for Jesus Christ.

Motives (Why we do what we do)

1. We are a **worshipping community** . . . because God created us and desires us to be in relationship with Him and others.

2. We are a **missional community** . . . because our world needs a demonstration of God's forgiving and healing love in words and actions.

3. We are an **inclusive community** . . . because following Jesus demands we overcome barriers of gender, language, race, class, age, and culture.

4. We are a **generous community** . . . because of our gratitude for the giving nature of God.

5. We are a **just community** . . . because following Jesus involves confronting the world's evils and restoring biblical truth (or justice).

Method (How we do what we do)
Step One: Develop Relationships
Step Two: Strengthen Relationships
Step Three: Serve in Relationships
Step Four: Partner in Service

Measures (When we will know we are successful)

1. When we are ministering *with* "all people" and not just ministering *to* "all people."
2. When our congregation is increasingly engaged in CROSS (cultural) training.
3. When local leaders seek our church for answers to community issues.

The development of this vision frame was a five-month process carried out by a dedicated group of leaders within the church. Many thanks to this team of seven: Becky Akana, Verdi Avila, Jim Reason, Leland Strange, Charles Summerour, Willard Smith, and Ian Waller.

APPENDIX C

▼ ▼ ▼

English as a Second Language (ESL)

Joy Goodman, Director

E SL is a vital part of First Baptist Church Duluth's strategy to reach the nations with the gospel of Jesus Christ. Classes are geared for adults, but an occasional high school student enrolls. Some students are Christians, but many have little or no church affiliation, and some have identified themselves as Muslim or Hindu.

The English skill level of the students varies tremendously, allowing for five different grades of classes. The Foundations Class is for students with no English proficiency. Levels one through three are focused on grammar, and level four is geared to help highly fluent students become comfortable in day-to-day interactions by expanding their vocabulary and introducing idioms.

The ESL faculty is all volunteers. A common misconception is that an ESL teacher needs to be a teaching professional and speak multiple languages. Our teachers come from a variety of vocational backgrounds; only one is a professional teacher and almost all of them speak only English. Training is provided to teachers through our denominational literacy mission. The only three requirements of every volunteer are to love God, to desire to serve people, and to speak English.

The class of 2016 has enrolled 123 students to date from twenty-four different countries and territories who speak sixteen different heart languages.

ESL Students' Birth Countries

Armenia

Brazil

China

Columbia

Cuba

Dominican Republic

El Salvador

Guatemala

Honduras

India

Iran

Italy

Japan

Jordan

Korea

Lithuania

Mexico

Myanmar

Puerto Rico (USA)

Russia

Taiwan

Turkmenistan

Venezuela

Vietnam

ESL Students' Heart Languages

Arabic	Karen
Armenian	Korean
Burmese	Lithuanian
Farsi	Mandarin
Hindi	Portuguese
Gujarati	Russian
Italian	Spanish
Japanese	Vietnamese

▼ ▼ ▼

Weekday Preschool

SoYoung Lee, Director

2016 Student Body Ethnicity

Anglo-American	24%
Korean	21%
South Asian (India/Pakistan)	16%
Chinese	9%
African-American	7%
Hispanic/Latino	7%
Vietnamese	6%
Japanese	4%
Romanian	1%
Polish/Lithuanian	1%
Cross-Cultural Families	4%

APPENDIX E

▼ ▼ ▼

One Initiative Projects Completed 2014–2016

*O*ne *Initiative* was a generosity campaign designed to generate additional funds beyond the regular budget receipts for the purpose of creating an atmosphere of inclusion and singularity of purpose in the church body. The initiative was based on John 17:22–23.

> I have given them the glory that you gave me, that they may be *one* as we are *one*—I in them and you in me—so that they be brought to *complete unity*. Then the world will know that you sent me and have loved them even as you have loved me. (NIV, emphasis mine)

The *One Initiative* was a catalyst for uniting the church around our purpose statement for the fulfillment of our ministry goals. Twelve *One Initiative* projects were completed from 2014 to 2016.

1. *The Dick Baker Ministry Learning Center*
New Orleans Baptist Theological Seminary opened an extension campus at First Baptist Church Duluth in August 2014.

Bachelor's and master's level classes are taught at the church. FBCD also houses the offices and library for the Korean Training Institute of NOBTS. The classrooms were equipped and dedicated in memory of our recently deceased Pastor Emeritus, Rev. Dick Baker.

2. *Blessings in a Backpack*
    FBCD provided needed backpacks and school supplies at the beginning of each school year for underprivileged families at our local elementary schools.

3. *Kid's Theater Remodel*
    The children's worship area received a needed facelift and name change with the opening of the new Kid's Theater.

4. *Feed the Need*
    Funds were provided to assist in the preparation of Thanksgiving dinners for over one hundred Duluth families. These dinners were delivered by volunteer teams on Thanksgiving morning.

5. *Youth Discipleship Areas*
    Living room furnishings provide an "at home" atmosphere for small group discipleship throughout the youth area.

6. *Preschool Playground*
    A state-of-the-art preschool playground was established for the weekday preschool as well as Sunday usage.

7. *Preschool Entry Remodel*

An aesthetically pleasing entryway was developed to engage preschoolers and their parents including a fish tank and a God's creation theme.

8. *Sound Booth Relocation/ Translation Booth Development*

The sound and lighting booth was moved from the sanctuary balcony to the floor level, providing much needed enhancement of sound technologies. The original sound booth was repurposed into four translation booths, providing opportunities for live interpretation during worship services.

9. *Youth Soda Shop*

A youth soda shop and snack bar was constructed and equipped for usage before and after youth activities.

10. *New Signage*

Outdoor and indoor signage was enhanced to better communicate with first-time guests.

11. *Great Commission Offering*

A significant gift was made to the church's annual missionary budget named *The Great Commission Offering*. (Note: this gift allowed the 2014 year to be the largest mission offering in the 130-year history of the church.)

12. *International Grounds Café*

A coffeehouse featuring international coffees was constructed and developed with all proceeds going to aid third-world church planting efforts.

The *One Initiative* campaign provided almost $300,000 beyond budget receipts to accomplish these projects.

▼ ▼ ▼

Population Trends for the City of Duluth[41]

	2000 Population	2013 Population	Change +/-
White/ Caucasian	64.2%	39.5%	-24.7%
Asian	12.8%	25.9%	+13.1%
Black	11.7%	18.8%	+ 7.1%
Hispanic	9.0%	12.9%	+ 3.9%
2 or More Ethnicities	1.8%	1.9%	+ 0.1%
Other	0.5%	1.0%	+ 1.0%

APPENDIX G

▼ ▼ ▼

First Baptist Church Planting Partners

India

Kakinada. . . . . Valluri Santhibabu. 2011–2013
(2 Villages: Yerrampalem, Katravulapalli)

Kakinada. . . . . Madey Ravindrababu. 2011–2013
(2 Villages: Rachael Peta, Ambajipeta)

Amritsar . . . . .Peter Hans. 2013–present
Bhopal. . . . . Samuel Rahm. 2014–present

Mexico

Solforino. . . . . .Pastor Leonardo Gil. 2012
Tres Reyes. . . . . Pastor Moises Chuc Hau. 2013
San Luis Potosi. . . . Josue Antonio Arellano. 2014–present

Nigeria

Fada Village Church ..... Samuel Ojewole......2016–present
(Supporting 11 Church Planters)

China

Underground Church.......... John Cao... Future Partners
Planting

United States

Duluth, MN .... Chuck Gilbert,
                    Hope Baptist Church......2013–present
Cumming, GA ....Andy Hall,
                    Redemption City Church......2014–present
(Metro Atlanta)

Sandy Springs, GA...Sam Dula/Will Kratt,
                    Perimeter Pointe......2015–present
(Metro Atlanta)

Summary: Supported twenty-three church planters in twenty-four
cities/villages representing five countries since 2011

Notes

1. See https://www.census.gov/newsroom/press-releases/2015/cb15-tps16.html.

2. Russell Moore, "A White Church No More," *New York Times*, May 6, 2016.

3. Dr. Jim Slack with the IMB taught on *urbanization* and *immigration* in a Great Commission Seminar at First Baptist Church Jonesboro, Georgia in October 2011.

4. Ibid.

5. Adapted from John Piper's book *Let the Nations Be Glad!* (Grand Rapids, MI: Baker Academic, 1993, 2003, 2010), 178–79.

6. David Platt, *Radical Together* (Colorado Springs, CO: Multnomah Books, 2011), 85.

7. Sermon preached at First Baptist Church Duluth on October 31, 2011.

8. Dr. Wayne Schmidt, lecture at the National Multi-Ethnic Conference in Long Beach, CA, November 5–6, 2013.

9. Story told in *Creating Community: 5 Keys to Building a Small Group Culture* by Andy Stanley and Bill Willits (Colorado Springs, CO: Multnomah Press, 2004), 19–20.

10. The church mission statement is the beginning of a complete "vision frame" formulated by a vision team to answer four critical questions: What do we do? (Mission); Why do we do what we do? (Motives); How do we do what we do? (Methods); When will we

know that we are successful? (Measures) An overview of the complete vision frame is found in Appendix B.

11. Max Lucado, *A Gentle Thunder* (Nashville, TN: Thomas Nelson, 1995), 115.

12. George H. W. Bush Interview, Academy of Achievement: Print Preview. See http://prodloadbalancer-1055872027.us-east-1.elb.amazonaws.com/autodoc/printmember/bus0int-1.

13. John Phillips, *Exploring Ephesians and Philippians,* The John Phillips Commentary Series (Grand Rapids, MI: Kregel Academic, 2nd edition, 2002).

14. Kadmiel's testimony about coming to the church is found in chapter 10.

15. Bab and Ulu's testimony is in chapter 10.

16. Jim Denison, "Church Is Not Important," *The Christian Post*, April 2, 2014.

17. Ed Stetzer, "Dropouts and Disciples," *Christianity Today*, May 14, 2014.

18. Audrey Barrick, "Evangelicals Lesser Known than Homosexuals," *The Christian Post*, June 26, 2008.

19. 2010 US Census data

20. Conversation with Dr. Jim Haskell, NAMB Atlanta Send City Coordinator.

21. Maynard Eaton, "Atlanta Is No.1 Hub for Human Trafficking," *Atlanta Daily World*, November 14, 2012.

22. Leonard Sweet, *The Gospel According to Starbucks: Living with a Grande Passion* (Colorado Springs, CO: WaterBrook Press, 2007).

23. John Phillips, *Exploring Romans,* The John Phillips Commentary Series (Grand Rapids, MI: Kregel Academic, 2nd edition, 2002), 202.

24. See Appendix A for a complete list.

25. First Baptist Church Duluth is mentioned in Laura Meckler's well-written article "How Churches Are Slowly Becoming Less Segregated," *Wall Street Journal*, published October 13, 2014.

26. Missionary Biography, William Carey: India, 1793–1834, at www.wholesomewords.org.

27. I heard this analogy in a sermon by Pastor Adrian Rogers more than twenty years ago.

28. Joshua Sharp, "On a Mission for Diversity," *Gwinnett Daily Post*, published July 31, 2015; http://www.gwinnettdailypost.com/archive/on-a-mission-for-diversity-duluth-church-adds-members-from/article_21727f8b-4bea-5fad-aa0f-96569a77cae8.html.

29. "Solve for X," *Elementary*, aired October 3, 2013.

30. Louise Radnofsky, "Illegal Immigrants Get Public Health Care," *Wall Street Journal*, published March 24, 2016.

31. Verdi was elected a deacon of First Baptist Church in 2012. He and two others elected that year were the first international-born men to be elected in the 130-year history of the church. Since then, five additional internationals have been elected to the deacon body.

32. Tom and Cindy Rhe are both graduates of Liberty University in Lynchburg, Virginia. Tom is currently pursuing a second master's degree with the Korean Training Institute of the New Orleans Baptist Theological Seminary. Classes are taught at First Baptist Church Duluth.

33. Roberto served as an ordained youth pastor in Mexico prior to coming to the United States. He met his wife, Jazmin, when both were serving as camp counselors at a Hispanic Summer Youth Ministry Camp. Jazmin serves as one of our Spanish interpreters through the One Voice Interpretation Center on Sunday mornings.

34. SoYoung is the first ever international-born ministry staff member of FBCD. She, her husband, K. J., and their daughters, Claire and Caitlyn, have moved to Duluth from the Dallas, Texas,

area at tremendous personal sacrifice, because they believe profoundly in the vision of FBCD.

35. Kadmiel is the vice president of Good News Centre, overseeing their United States fundraising efforts. He serves as a deacon and on the Missions Committee at FBCD. His wife, Isoleth, leads the church's Indian Dance Team.

36. Donald A. McGavran, *Understanding Church Growth* (Grand Rapids, MI: Wm. B. Eerdmans, 1970, 1980, 1993), 46.

37. Korie L. Edwards, Brad Christerson, and Michael O. Emerson, "Race, Religious Organizations, and Integration," *Annual Review of Sociology* Vol. 39 (2013): 211–28.

38. Mark DeYmaz and Harry Li, *Leading a Healthy Multi-Ethnic Church* (Grand Rapids, MI: Zondervan, 2010), 25–26.

39. Ibid., 28.

40. Edwards, Christerson, Emerson, "Race, Religious Organizations, and Integration," 211–28.

41. Data gathered from www.city-data.com. Census Bureau reports Duluth's population was 60 percent smaller in 1990 and was 91 percent White/Caucasian.